NEVER ENDING
ADVENTURE

NEVER ENDING ADVENTURE

Lowell Sheppard
with
Catherine Butcher

CROSSWAY BOOKS
Nottingham

Copyright © 1993 by Lowell Sheppard

First edition 1993

ISBN 1 85684 049 2

Typeset by Avocet Typesetters, Bicester, Oxon
Printed in the United Kingdom for Crossway Books,
Norton Street, Nottingham by
Cox & Wyman Ltd, Reading, Berks

Acknowledgements and Dedication

With thanks to: Helen Share, Sharon Roberts and Heather Parry for their help with typing; Stephen Gaukroger and Bill Hogg for their help and advice; Peter and Shirley Ling who provided a half-way point for Catherine and I to meet as we began to write this book; my Mum, Dad and Grandmother, who helped me recall the early years; Kande, along with Ryan and Mackenzie, for all they mean to me; Adrian Butcher and Jenny Moore for their prayers and encouragement and Gerard Kelly for research in Croatia.

Dedication: To Luke Sheppard and Millie Butcher whose brief lives have shaped our adventures.

(Note: Some names have been changed to protect the identity of some individuals)

Contents

Foreword

I am always highly suspicious of people who, when dealing with matters of faith, talk as if they have arrived. They seem to convey a feeling that if one follows a certain formula, then everything will be OK. In this context, faith is certainly not seen as a journey. To my mind, this thinking is not only unhelpful but also unbiblical.

Some years ago, an Australian Bible teacher (mentioned a few times in this book!) told me, 'you cannot be disillusioned unless you're suffering from an illusion'. Hearing those words and understanding them probably saved me from having to call myself an ex-believer. So much of what we are fed and taught today by the world is illusory; the church often plays the same game by embracing a quick fix, easy answer theology that leaves many alienated and disillusioned.

Lowell's journey as told in this book will be a great help to those folk. It is refreshing to find someone being honest and vulnerable, qualities sadly absent from many preachers these days. Strangely enough, like Lowell, it was in Thailand that I first realised that I hadn't found what I was looking for and I've been grateful every day since. I still haven't and this book is a wonderful confirmation that I'm in good company and on the right road.

Martyn Joseph
March 1993

Prologue

Midnight, Leicester Square, London

Bruce Springsteen was right when he said 'everyone has a hungry heart'.

An 'awareness evening' in Britain's capital confirms Springsteen's assessment of the human spirit.

The images acquired tonight provoke reflection: seedy clubs in Soho, homeless of all ages sleeping rough on the Strand, and teenagers high on hormones seeking adventure in state of the art video arcades featuring Quasar and Virtual Reality.

My colleagues continue on to King's Cross to join a team working with prostitutes. I am leaving earlier than the rest due to a viral infection that has plagued me for months.

My night on London streets concludes in conversation with a young man outside the Burger King.

Aided by a few pints, he declares honestly, 'I've had a h**l of a lot of pain in my life'. The words spark a train of thought that races me to other places, times and faces . . . a distressed seeker at the Glastonbury Festival, Britain's largest rave . . . Vincent, the wino in Liverpool . . . a family of thirty-five whose lives have been viciously interrupted by war in Yugoslavia . . . a farm worker from Yorkshire dreaming of adventure . . . and my own . . . all of us inexplicably linked by an aching void and a deep longing for meaning and purpose.

While debate rages about what has gone wrong with Western society, the most fundamental question continues to burn in the human spirit . . . 'Why am I here?'

The answer is revealed only to sojourners, restless hearts, people prepared to embark on a never ending journey of discovery!

Lowell Sheppard

1

Welcome to hell

War for me was only a nightmare. but for the family we stayed with in the Croatian town of Karlovac, it was a daily reality. As we shared a meal together in their home, Ladislav, a Baptist minister, told us his family's story. For several months they had been caught in the crossfire as Serb forces attempted to occupy their town. They knew that if they left their flat on the top floor of the church, the building might be closed and they could never return. They showed us pieces of shrapnel dug out of the walls; described sleepless nights crouched on the kitchen floor as bullets whistled through their windows; recounted tales of harrowing trips out to find food, crawling on all fours as mortars exploded only twenty feet away. A few hundred yards from their home a sign identified the beginning of the military zone. It read simply: 'Welcome to hell.'

Ladislav was pastor of the Karlovac Baptist Church; a man of about my age, living with his wife and six-year-old daughter in a frontline area in the conflict which engulfed Yugoslavia as it disintegrated. I live with my wife and two sons in the peaceful, picturesque heart of England. From Ladislav's home on the top floor of the Karlovac church, at one point in the war, he could see Serb troops from the living room window and Croat soldiers from the kitchen. The building, still scarred by shrapnel, was a food depot distributing aid to the thousands of refugees who have flooded into the area. My experiences of food shortages and homelessness have come only second-hand through visits to men like Ladislav. At home we always have enough to eat and can rest easy at night knowing our home is secure.

The visit to Karlovac was part of a four-man, fact-finding mission for Spring Harvest, Europe's largest Christian event. Our aim was to identify significant and strategic work being carried out through a Christian humanitarian project called 'My Neighbour'. As a result of the trip young people at Spring Harvest would be able to fund and equip a youth officer in a Croatian refugee camp to focus on the spiritual, emotional and physical needs of children and teenagers made homeless by the war.

During the three-day visit we were shocked to meet families who had been driven from their homes, not by the army, but by their own neighbours. We saw evidence of professional armies at war and worse: of a tide of ethnic hatred which was provoking acts of unprecedented inhumanity. As well as meeting Ladislav we met the Bozics, a family of thirty-five spanning three generations who stayed in one three-bedroomed house for six months until beds were found elsewhere. A Croatian Roman Catholic family, they had lived at peace with their Serbian neighbours for years until April 1992 when they were told: 'It is time for you to go.' With only a few minutes warning, they abandoned their homes and belongings and walked through the mountains for nineteen hours to reach the Croatian border. As they left, their neighbours erected a barrier across their property warning that any Croatian found on the wrong side would be killed. They had every reason to believe the threat as, a few months earlier, one brother was found six days after being beaten and left for dead: his jaw, arms and legs had been broken in several places and his cheek had been pierced by the barrel of a gun. Other brothers, fighting in Bosnia, reported that the family home had been burned to the ground, yet they still clung to the hope that one day they would go home. Meanwhile they were dependent on aid offered by Moj Blezni – My Neighbour – an evangelical humanitarian organisation set up in direct response to the war and ensuing refugee crisis.

We were introduced to 'My Neighbour' by Baptist Pastor Stevo Dereta who, like everyone we met, had his own stories of suffering and hardship to tell. When we arrived in the Adriatic port of Rijeka, Stevo had just returned from a trip into Bosnia to bring out a pastor and his family. Their fourth child had been born just five days earlier. They had minimal food and medical care and had been reduced to burning books to keep warm.

Stevo spoke of the war as a crucible for the church: a test on which the whole future of evangelical Christianity in Croatia might rest. If Christians were seen to be helping their neighbours at their time of crisis, there would be open doors later to talk about the source of all hope – Jesus Christ. But 'My Neighbour' was offering aid, first and foremost, out of love; finding recognition in Croatian society would be a welcome by-product. Visiting the 'My Neighbour' warehouse we were again confronted with the personal tragedy which faced its workers each day. The three-storey building had been donated to 'My Neighbour' by a church member whose wife met us as we arrived to see the project's nerve-centre. She had just discovered that her two brothers had been killed in Bosnia. Death and separation scarred the lives of everyone we met.

From the warehouse, with its stacks of tins, bags of potatoes and boxes of clothes awaiting distribution through a network of local churches, we drove to a refugee camp. Formerly a work camp for the teams which built the roads into Rijeka, it was a spartan site with six wooden huts which had become home to 400 people. Hajic Hussein, one of the few men in the camp, told us that his three sons were in concentration camps. Their wives and children were separated. When the conflict began their town was the scene of hand-to-hand fighting between Serbs and Croats. Hundreds died on both sides, but then more heavily armed Serb troops moved in to take control. At that point Hajic's relatives and 800 other Muslim families, were forced from their homes. It was almost impossible to empathise with the awful plight of the refugees we met who had seen their property destroyed and their lives interrupted. At the refugee camp Stevo gave out apples to the children. It was chaos as the youngsters fought with each other for these free gifts. I had to walk away until I could bring my emotions under control.

Serving God is an adventure, but was this the adventure I was looking for? In Croatia I saw God's adventurers at work using practical and spiritual gifts to demonstrate God's kingdom. I saw how suffering and hardship are hallmarks of the adventurer's lifestyle, rather than romance or daring deeds. As I sensed deep peace in men like Ladislav, in spite of the trauma of life in the frontline, I realised again how those who draw on God's resources are the world's real heroes; vain human efforts are weak and pathetic in comparison.

Part of my adventure has been discovering how God equips and prepares us for the tasks he plans for us to do. The adventures he has taken me through are not those I'd have planned. Often, it is only with hindsight that I have traced God's hand at work turning some testing times into training, and hardship into hurdles to be overcome. My roots as an adventurer began with my pioneering grandfather, one of the early settlers who left England to become a farmer in the vast Canadian Prairies. He knew little of God, but was hungry for adventure. God met him in middle age and his death-bed dream was for a family of pioneers in God's kingdom. That dream was the beginning of a never-ending adventure, first for my father and then for me.

2

Pioneers

Harry Sheppard had never made an important decision. His life had been marked by boring predictability. As a farm labourer his future had been mapped out for him. Now, however, he was facing a decision that would catapult him out of his humdrum existence. Born in Leeds during years of economic depression, he was 23 and had few prospects. It was an election year in the USA. There was political unrest in Serbia; liberation movements forming in Russia; and in Britain, unemployment was high and rising. Factories were closing. New technology was making growing numbers of workers redundant. As a farm-hand he had watched grain prices plummet as cheap imports forced prices down.

His story could be that of many unskilled workers today. But Harry – my grandfather – was living in 1904 when Edward VII was on the British throne. Although I don't know much about my grandfather, I am confident that he was a man hungry for adventure.

The Great Depression had taken its toll, but all was not gloom and despondency. There was a spirit of optimism and adventure in many hearts. The Wright brothers had made their first flight in a prototype airplane the previous year and Henry Ford had just founded his famous motor company. The Panama Canal was under construction, and there was talk of a Channel Tunnel. Thousands of Europeans were heading for new territories in the Americas, lured by the promise of free land. Between 1881 and 1915, 36 million Europeans emigrated; and two and a half million found their way to Canada.

Canada beckoned my adventure-seeking grandfather and his brother Ted. The advertisements said some of the best land in the world was there for the taking. All a man needed was a $10 filing fee to stake a claim on 160 acres of government land. The pamphlets portrayed Saskatchewan as the promised land of plenty. In three years you could have your own apple and peach orchards and fields of waving grain where the yield was the highest in the world. The leaflets were obviously not written by anyone who had visited Saskatchewan, but the propaganda worked. After all, land was precious to Europeans and the possibility of being a landowner was bait to many people like Grandpa.

He and Ted set sail from England and arrived in their new world in 1905 ignorant of the severe winters which grew so cold barbed wire fences would snap; apple and peach orchards were merely advertising hype. The reality was harsh and austere. I'm sure my grandpa must have felt conned when he eventually arrived at his homestead.

They travelled by train from Toronto to Winnipeg, where they were given a small pouch with soil from the land that was to be theirs. To stake a claim Grandpa had to pay the filing fee, then had to live on the land for six months of each year for three years, breaking ten acres a year. His land was 60 miles south of Regina, near Pangman, Saskatchewan, and getting there involved an arduous 400 mile journey west by covered wagon. They travelled across the Canadian Prairies clutching their pouch of sample soil. Every westward mile reinforced the cruelty of the con-trick he had fallen prey to.

Grandpa began to build his homestead in June 1905. The house was basic; just sods of earth made into a shack.

The work was back-breaking; in his first year he tackled only five acres. In 1906 he acquired two horses and broke 15 acres that year and the next. When his three years were up, assuring his ownership of the land, he returned to England to visit his family. He must have felt like giving up many times, but he made it; he had climbed his Everest; the peasant had become a landowner.

He returned to Canada with new-found confidence. On his return trip in 1909 romance blossomed on board ship. The woman who captured his heart was Mary Nendick, also Yorkshire-born, from a family of twelve. Like many of her contemporaries, Mary had been in domestic service before leaving England for new hope and freedom in Canada. British suffragettes were becoming militant back in England, but Mary's trip was not an act of defiance. Her family life was unhappy and she'd been encouraged to emigrate to find a new life. She never talked about why she left and she never returned to her North Yorkshire home.

Grandpa proposed to her before they left the ship, though they went their separate ways. Mary stayed in Toronto, while Grandpa returned to his homestead. They corresponded for three years and were married at Christmas-time in 1912 at All Saints Church, Toronto. When they did move back west they settled in Manor for a year where Grandpa ran a general store. It was there that their daughter Jean was born.

Two years passed before they finally returned to the homestead in 1916 to farm a few pigs and chickens and to grow their main money-earner, wheat. Soon there were more children; Mary, named after her mother and then George, named after Lloyd George, the British wartime Prime Minister.

My grandfather was interested in politics and became a member of the Canadian Liberal Party, standing as a local councillor in Pangman. He was described by fellow councillors as 'a valued and much respected member of the council'. Politics expressed his concern for his community but did not change his life. The life of the whole family did change dramatically when, in 1920, they moved a few miles south to Black Oak. No one knows precisely what made Grandpa sell his homestead in 'Sheppard Coolie,' the name given to it by the Saskatchewan government. Maybe Grandpa didn't know either. But they were strangely drawn to Black Oak, several miles away.

Unknown to them, a huge tent had been pitched in Black Oak and people were flocking from miles around each night to hear forthright preaching from the Bible and to see for themselves whether the rumours of spectacular demonstrations of the power of God were true. Sometimes meetings went on all night long as men confessed their sin and got right with God and with their fellow men.

It was the real 'hell-fire and brimstone' preaching that was so typical of the early Pentecostal movement in Canada, accompanied by miracles and acts of mercy. Such was the attraction that people would travel twenty to thirty miles to attend the meetings; no mean feat in a covered wagon, particularly when the cows had to be milked at 5am the morning after.

When the tent moved on from Black Oak, local people whose lives had been so dramatically changed by God continued to meet in Black Oak School. My grandparents moved to a homestead right next to the school. Their house was on the very piece of land where the tent had been pitched. My family were not practising Christians. My grandmother was quite superstitious and would read tea-leaves. Little did they know what they had moved into!

At first, Grandpa was attracted by the singing. He would go to the front door and listen to the music wafting across the fields. Sometimes he and Grandma walked down past the school so they could hear better. Finally they went into a meeting. That may have been the first time they had ever heard of God's love.

At first they were frightened by the fire and brimstone fervour of the revivalist preaching. One night after the preaching, an invitation was given to go forward and surrender to God. My grandmother was terrified and fled from the meeting with her baby in her arms. But one of the ladies ran after her and, taking the baby, encouraged Grandma not to be scared, but rather to give her life to God. Within a short time my grandfather also surrendered to God and the whole family started to attend the meetings regularly. They had been well and truly converted.

Throughout the 1920s, as other pioneers around the world crossed new frontiers such as flying to the North Pole, inventing television or discovering penicillin, my grandparents were discovering a new dimension to life as they grew in their new-found faith. Two brothers from England and a Scottish farmer became pastors of the church that had been established; they were committed to teaching the truth from the Bible, applying it to everyday life.

During that decade three more sons were born; Jim in 1923 and David in 1925. Arthur, my father, arrived in 1928, kicking and screaming. Even before he was born, my father was prayed for and dedicated to God. His birth marked the completion of the family.

Life on the land was never easy. Winter temperatures plummeted to 40°C below freezing. In the summer, crops shrivelled in the searing heat, but they had learned what the land could yield and knew when to plant and harvest. The family were well respected in the community. Grandpa became a local councillor in 1928 and served for four years. The family always had clothes to wear, though only the basic essentials. They had no Sunday suits but Grandma wanted the family to be clean and presentable for church. She put the children to bed early on Saturday night so that she could wash and dry their overalls.

They never went hungry, but the food was plain. Chocolate cake was only on offer at Charlie White's farm. The White's were the Sheppard's well-to-do neighbours and the Sheppard children were often on the receiving end of their Christian kindness. Mrs White regularly treated the little Sheppards to freshly-baked cookies or slices of cake. These delights were washed down with enormous glasses of milk. The White's car was always packed on trips to church or Christian camps. They ensured that the Sheppard children didn't miss out. The children of both families were of similar age; young Arthur Sheppard even shared a school desk with young John Wesley White, who was later to become an associate of Billy Graham following studies at Oxford.

As the Roaring Twenties turned to the depression of the Thirties, life took a sharp turn for the worse. On 30 November 1931 the Sheppard family home burned to the ground. A visitor saw smoke, but thought it was simply steam, rising from the back of the house. When Grandpa went to investigate the house was already well alight. The timber frame burned quickly and the house was totally gutted. The family was safe, but could only spectate as their possessions went up in smoke. Grandpa was quoted as saying: 'It's a terrible thing to watch your house burn.' All he had worked for materially since 1905 was devoured by fire that night.

The family moved in with neighbours for the first week after the fire. Then, friends in the community rallied round and helped them set up home in the mission house. It was a bleak Christmas but, by the following spring, they had built a much smaller house on land where the revival meeting tent had been pitched. I remember this house as my Uncle David and his family lived in it until the 1960s. It is now used as a chicken coop on their farm.

Sadly, my grandfather did not live to enjoy his new home. He was diagnosed as suffering from cancer. Early in 1932 he had surgery, then in March went for further treatment at the Mayo Clinic in Rochester, Minnesota. He returned home, but the family could see his strength was ebbing away. Christian friends came from miles around to see him. My father remembers: 'May 25th arrived and there was an unusual stillness in the house as the three smallest boys were called to his bedside. He spoke to us, expressing his desire that we would be good to Mother and that we would live godly lives.'

During the day neighbours came to say goodbye to him and one of the men heard him praying that if God healed him, he would be an evangelist. But if that was not the Father's will, he asked God to use one of his children as an evangelist to tell others the Good News of Jesus Christ.

My father recalls: 'At six that evening, with my mother sitting by his bedside, he bade her farewell, and told her he could see Jesus standing by her, waiting to take him. In a few moments, with the praises of God on his lips, he died. Mother felt the presence of God around the bed, so much so that she claimed to see angels ascending and descending over his death bed.'

Grandpa was buried three days later in the village cemetery. Again neighbours rallied round and seeded the crop which, when harvested, proved to be plentiful. Family photographs reveal a change in Grandma's face around this time. Her eyes had always sparkled with hope, but Grandpa's death and the harsh life which followed took their toll. Sadness and fatigue made their mark. Although the Mayo Clinic waived their bill, there were other debts to pay. The bank was knocking on the door for money, so Grandma had to write to the bank manager pleading for mercy. She never got it and turned to her family for help.

Support came from Big Jim, a relative who helped her run the farm for a while. Even with Big Jim around it was a very difficult time for her. Grandma felt humiliated by her dependence on people's charity, but her faith in God didn't waiver. Family prayers were always part of the daily pattern of life.

From early childhood my father was part of the Sunday School where he memorised passages from the Bible and learned about the Christian life. As he grew older, fiery evening sermons on hell, judgement and the cross challenged him. But when my grandmother heard him singing his favourite hymn: 'When the roll is called up yonder I'll be there' and asked 'Are you sure you'll be there?' he realised that he couldn't live on his parents' faith but had to surrender his own life to Christ. He was only about nine years old when he made the decision that would affect his entire life.

It was not until he moved away from the homestead that my father's Christian commitment was really put to the test. At the age of 16 he left home to study accountancy at a college in Regina, 60 miles to the north. Sundays included church, but he says, 'I wanted the rest of the week to myself to look around a little and broaden my mind.' His first taste of the big, wide world went against all he had been taught.

In those days cinemas were no-go areas for good, clean-living Christian young men. But, defiantly, my father decided to go to see a film about Mark Twain's character Tom Sawyer. I laugh now when I think of it, but Dad had heard preachers condemning cinemas and felt incredibly guilty. He was going against his conscience and, even before the film ended, he was overcome with guilt and left, vowing that he would never set foot in a cinema again. He asked God's forgiveness and began to develop a living relationship with Jesus Christ, though he felt there was something missing in his Christian life.

I am fascinated by the Christianity of the 1930s in Canada. God moved powerfully in signs, wonders and anointed preaching, but there was also a denial of the goodness of creation; only eternal things mattered. Sadly this false dualism still pervades much of the Canadian church. You now find cinemas full of Christians, but they view the screen uncritically.

In church, Dad found that the other young people were much bolder than he was. When he was invited to a Bible Convention at Lake Katepwa, he went, but when he was asked to give his 'testimony' he felt it was very weak compared to the other young people's stories. On the last night of the camp others were praying fervently while, Dad says, his prayers seemed feeble.

'It was after midnight when we gathered under the

canvas and the boys prayed with great boldness and sincerity, pouring out their hearts to God. Kneeling all by myself towards the front of the tent, I began very feebly to praise the Lord, asking him to give me the same power and boldness. Suddenly I began to feel the presence of God, and it seemed that my whole body began to tremble as the feeling, like an electric shock, went through my entire body.

'As the moments passed, the glory of God seemed to grow stronger, until I could not help but begin to praise God. I knew it was coming right from my heart, gushing from my soul until I could not express myself any longer in the English language. Suddenly I was speaking in a language which I had never been taught. As I spoke the words, Christ became more real. I had no doubt it was of God.

'The moments quickly turned to hours. There came a fierce preoccupation with those who don't know Christ. Never in my whole life had I experienced such a deep concern for those dying without Jesus. It seemed that nothing was more important than to win people to Christ. I caught a vision of millions outside of Christ, dying without hope, and somehow I felt that Christ was calling me to surrender everything, so that I might preach about him. It seemed that I could see multitudes waiting with outstretched arms for the message of life. That night at 3.30am I asked God to take all of me and use me. I knew without a doubt that I was to preach the Gospel of Christ.'

Grandpa's prayer was being answered.

3

Footsteps to follow

Determined to follow the example of the apostle Paul and to remain single, my father met with a surprise at college where he began training to become an ordained minister. A girl called Greta Ramsay visited the Bible School to be a bridesmaid at a friend's wedding and decided to enrol. When the students took turns to wash the dishes after meals my father's hand touched Greta's as they worked in the soapy water. That touch must have broken his resolve. He wrote a few years later: 'My heart seemed strangely moved, and I just couldn't seem to control the feelings that went on inside. I prayed much, but it seemed that I could not get rid of the strange feeling that had come over my life toward this new first year student.'

I'm sure that his desire to follow Paul was a cover for his shyness and awkwardness with girls, but love conquers even shyness. Three months passed before he put his feelings into words. It was the day after his graduation from college. 'It took much help from the Lord to restrain our feelings one for another, for our hearts were being knit together, and we soon knew that we were meant for one another.'

My father spent the following summer working with evangelistic teams all over western Canada. But by

Christmas he and Greta were re-united. He met her family for the first time and, on New Year's afternoon, took her out for a drive. When they stopped at the end of a lonely road he says, 'I took her hand and together we prayed. Then I asked her that all-important question. I asked her if she would be happy to be my wife. She answered yes without any hesitation and we praised God together.'

Deep down my father is a bit of a romantic; however my mother has a mischievous streak which I'm said to have inherited. Years after they married, when Dad arrived home after midnight having spent the evening at a particularly stressful church board meeting, Mum was waiting for him. When she leapt out at him in the darkened hall, wearing a monster mask, they woke the whole house!

They were married in Vancouver on 1st October 1949. My father wrote later: 'We dedicated our lives to world evangelism. After our honeymoon at White Rock, we set out on our mission'.

My mother's family had been established in Canada for several generations, though they too had emigrated from Europe. My maternal grandmother, Martha Douglas, came from Nova Scotia; her ancestors had been some of the early settlers from Glasgow, Scotland; my mother's father, Anton Stromstead, was from Norway.

When their first child was about six months old, my grandmother became pregnant again. Three months later, their first baby died; it was on 26 June 1928, the date my own first child was born many years later. When her baby died my grandmother says she didn't allow herself to grieve because of the life within her. The second baby that was born six months later was my mother, Greta.

At the time my grandmother believed in God but now admits that she didn't know God. She went into labour on 31 December 1928 but the doctor was at a New Year's Eve party and couldn't come to deliver the baby. So, to slow her contractions, they gave her ether.

My mother was delivered by the doctor, still wearing his black tuxedo, at 12.01 on New Year's Day 1929; the birth got a special mention in the *Edmonton Journal* of 2 January.

When my grandmother told me about the news she began to cry because it had given her such incredible happiness. Up to that point her life had been really mixed up. Anton wasn't a good husband. He was often drunk and violent. And, although she had no firm faith of her own, God demonstrated his love for her by giving her Greta. The experience sparked Grandma's conversion and it wasn't too long after the birth of my mother that she decided to become a Christian.

Another baby, called Gloria, was born a couple of years later. Three days before Gloria's birth Anton Stromstead left them; they didn't see him again for decades. My mother was a different child, Grandma says. For some reason Gloria was the family favourite and my mother was often left out. The situation worsened when my mother was about four as Grandma divorced Anton and married a man called Hector Ramsay. Grandma had two more daughters by Hector. My mother felt even more isolated.

Mum's childhood wasn't pleasant, but there was a sense of God's calling on her life. A local pastor invited my grandmother to send her children to Sunday School. Mum was only five years old but recalls: 'As a result, I learned of Jesus' love and gave my life to him, kneeling by a red chair as the teacher led me in a prayer.'

Seven years later a couple called Mr and Mrs Moses held a mission at the church and Mum remembers hearing God say: 'One day you will be doing what they are doing.' But when she left home to work in Vancouver, she left her faith and her family behind. Following in her father's footsteps she took to drink to relieve her pain and was well on the way to becoming an alcoholic.

In her late teens Mother came back to God. She was a member of a bowling league and took part in professional competitions. One day my grandmother, who had been praying for her, was going to a Christian event and asked my mother to help her carry some cakes to the meeting.

Mum agreed, though only if she could drop the cakes off and leave for her bowling competition. Mum says: 'I was sure that God was not interested in me any more and that even he would reject me as others had.'

When she arrived at the meeting there was a very tall, dark, handsome man at the door. He wasn't my father; in fact he's now one of my parents' best friends! My mother found him attractive and decided to stay for the meeting. Some of the young people she met spent time explaining that God wanted to receive and forgive her. She responded and says: 'I was instantly delivered of addiction to cigarettes and strong drink. My life was changed.'

She had missed her bowling tournament, but had found the love, acceptance and forgiveness she had been looking for. Nine months later when she went to be a bridesmaid at a wedding at Eston Bible College, she decided to stay on as a student. It was there she met my father and fell in love.

When Dad took Mum home to meet his mother my grandmother's private comment to my father was: 'She's nice but she's far too old for you!' She still saw my father as a little boy. But in fact my mother was well received by the family and the marriage has been a strong one.

Dad was already becoming a respected evangelist and began to get some good preaching opportunities. In his first mission at a big church in Regina, he was preaching when a young courting couple walked in. They came back to several mission meetings and, on the final night, they committed their lives to Christ. They married and later became students at Eston Bible College, and boarded with my parents for a year. (By then my father was lecturing at the college.) The couple, Thelma and Bill Bettschen are my wife Kande's parents.

That was all in the future. My parents' common goal was to share their faith and Europe was to be their first missionary adventure. At a Youth for Christ event in Ontario they heard Lorne Johannes outline YFC evangelism plans for Europe; British Youth for Christ had been started in 1947 by evangelists Billy Graham and Torrey Johnson.

Dad wrote: 'My heart was thrilled as he (Lorne Johannes) related the vision of this great world movement.'

When one of the evangelists said he felt my father should be one of the team to go to Europe it struck a chord. Dad needed $500 to cover the cost and, miraculously, the money he needed arrived in the next morning's post. On 21 June 1950 he set sail for France with a 40-strong YFC team. His itinerary took in Belgium, England, Germany and Italy. They preached to packed auditoriums and saw hundreds respond.

'We arrived home in Quebec, tired and worn, but grateful to God. We came home different than we went for our hearts were burdened and burning for the 400 million Europeans who needed to hear a message of hope,' my father said.

They made the next trip together in spite of my mother's initial fear of sailing. They had a calm crossing and docked at Greenock, Scotland. Their next port of call was Eastbourne on the English south coast where they stayed with the British Youth for Christ treasurer Lewis Ford.

As they prayed for Europe, Portugal was the country which was impressed on them, though they had no contact with the country. Forty-eight hours after agreeing in prayer that God was calling them to Portugal, they received a cable from YFC in Chicago saying: 'Proceed to Portugal.'

They set off immediately and, in the two months that they spent ministering in Portugal, they saw more than 300 people respond to Jesus Christ and many healed. From Portugal they travelled to Ireland, then Wales and Yorkshire, before they returned home in time for the birth of their first child, my sister Faith, on 21 June 1952.

They took a rest from travelling for a few months as Dad lectured at the Bible College in Eston, but that Christmas the threesome drove 2,000 miles to Texas for three weeks of preaching in San Antonio. Their prayers for Europe still focused on Portugal and, after returning to Vancouver plans slotted into place for my father to make a return trip, leaving Mum and Faith behind. The Crown Prince of Japan was also on board and during the Atlantic crossing Dad gave him a booklet called 'God's Way of Salvation'. In a letter thanking him for the gift, the Crown Prince said: 'I thank you for your kindness in including in your prayer your wishes for a happy trip. We all need to pray for our salvation, and your prayer is all the more highly appreciated.' No one could know the place Japan was to play in the family's future.

Once again the European trip saw many people become Christians and many healed both in Britain, where they docked, and then in Portugal.

While he was travelling he received an invitation from the Full Gospel Bible Institute in Eston to join the staff, training others. He accepted and on returning to Canada, Dad, Mum and Faith made their home at the Bible school, though vacations still found them travelling throughout Canada, the USA and even to Jamaica preaching and planting churches.

Today it's hard to go to any Full Gospel church in western Canada without finding someone who was converted or influenced by my father's ministry. He played a part in planting many churches. His first love is to preach the Gospel and he's still doing it! They didn't have much money. They faced hostility and even had their lives threatened. But they knew God had called them to do what they were doing and were constantly challenged to 'press on for God and to blaze new trails'. They lived a life of faith and adventure. They saw God provide miraculously on a regular basis, though they lived on a meagre income; on one mission they survived eating only rhubarb.

Shortly after they returned from a trip to Jamaica, on 20 March 1955, I was born in a make-shift hospital in Eston Town Hall. (The hospital had burned to the ground only a few weeks before.) My father was so excited about the imminent arrival of his second child that he drove my mother to the Town Hall without turning on the car's headlights; that is until he was stopped by an officer of the Royal Canadian Mounted Police! I made my debut at 3.15am and was named Lowell Ramsay Arthur: Lowell after a missionary friend Lowell Chandler who was working in Jamaica; Ramsay after my mother's step-father and Arthur after my father.

4

When I was a child . . .

By naming me Lowell, my father gave me a double challenge: to follow in the missionary footsteps of the man named Lowell Chandler whom he admired, and to overcome my speech impediment every time I introduce myself: Lowell is not an easy word to pronounce! I have a mild neurological disorder, called clutter, which means I talk too fast and run words into each other.

Learning to speak was one of my first major hurdles in life. I couldn't speak until I was three; all I said was 'ish', then I'd point at whatever I wanted. The day Faith, my sister, started school I said my first word: 'pop' (soda pop). Maybe my lack of speech was because Faith did all the talking for me. She was the only one who knew what I meant when I said 'ish'.

Having two children did not dent my parents' missionary zeal. In the autumn of 1956 they went to Cuba for six weeks, taking Faith but leaving me with Grandma Ramsay. It was the year before Fidel Castro began to gain power, though there had been unrest for some time. I was only 18 months old so world politics did not affect me. However I can remember sitting at a counter in Grandma's house eating a bowl of soup when my parents walked into the room after their trip. Instead of rushing to welcome them home, I cried and ran away. I didn't recognise them. My mother now regrets leaving me for so long at such a young age; she is concerned that it made a lasting impression on me.

Travelling was our way of life and from then on I went too. My father became Director of Youth for Christ, Saskatchewan in 1957 so he travelled a lot in that role. We bought our first house that year, in Moose Jaw. Ted Engstrom, who was appointed Chairman of Youth for Christ International in 1992, was also an evangelist with YFC in those days; he and my dad toured together that year.

In 1958 we moved to Vancouver on the West Coast of Canada and Dad became the evangelist at the Evangelistic Tabernacle, a prestigious church on Canada's west coast. He led mission meetings and planted churches in surrounding communities. Ern Baxter was the pastor who became known in Britain working with Bryn Jones as the Dales Bible Weeks got under way.

As a toddler, I have few specific memories. On one journey in our Volkswagen Van I was wrestling with my cousin Rod Crawford in the back of the van, when I hit the back doors and fell out. We were doing about thirty miles an hour. I landed on the tarmac and rolled into a ditch. My parents didn't discover I was missing until they had driven another mile down the road. Rod was in a state of shock and the van was very noisy so my disappearance had gone unnoticed, but when they looked back the van doors were open and I was gone.

They came back to find me and immediately took me to Granddad Ramsay's house a couple of miles away in Crescent Beach. My head was cut open and I was covered in blood. My mother and father said they'd never seen my grandfather pray with such fervour and faith. Doctors later told them it was a miracle that my injuries were not worse. I had mild concussion but no permanent damage. I have vivid memories of the accident; I sobbed broken-heartedly, not so much because I'd been injured, but because in falling out of the van I'd smashed my ukulele!

My brother Brent was born in 1960 at Whiterock where Dad was church-planting and, a year later, I started school there. But we were soon on the move again.

My second significant memory was when I was about five years old. My father was planting a church on Saltspring Island and for weeks on end I refused to sleep alone. Every night I saw, what I described as demons at the front window trying to get in.

I still have a vivid picture in my mind of these fuzzy, ethereal, ugly creatures hammering at the window. I could see them and hear them hammering so I couldn't figure out why my Dad couldn't see them too! I was terrified.

I still wonder how real they were or to what extent they were the product of a fertile imagination, but I do recognise that evil spirits are real; C.S. Lewis strikes a good balance in his view that it is equally dangerous to be paranoid about Satan's powers as to deny his activity. Satan is hell-bent on stopping people advancing in their adventure with God. He is real and I believe he even makes a bid for the lives of children. Parents' prayers are a sure safeguard though. My early teenage years were marred by a demonic darkness and I believe that the prayer of my mother, in particular, kept me safe during that period of rebellion . . . but more of that later.

We lived on Saltspring Island for about seven months until they could find a pastor to take over the church Dad had planted. Saltspring Island played an important part in my spiritual journey. While Dad was planting the church I heard the story of Jesus summoning grown men to give up their careers and, even though I was only five, I decided I too wanted to follow Jesus.

One day we had just finished Sunday School and my parents had invited everyone back to an 'open house' at our home on Saltspring Island. A man I called Uncle John who was our Sunday School teacher was helping my father take people back to the house. I was with some other kids packed into his Volkswagen Beetle, and, as we were driving along we began to talk about Jesus' challenge to follow him. I don't remember whether I initiated it, or Uncle John suggested that I obey Christ's call. But on that journey I made a decision to accept this Jesus we'd been talking about. Uncle John led me in a prayer and when we arrived at my parents' house I remember leaping out of the Volkswagen wanting to tell everyone what had happened.

I had prayed a prayer of commitment lots of times before then and felt that nothing had happened; in fact every time my father made an appeal in a mission meeting I would pray the prayer which he would say with those who had responded. Even as a youngster I was beginning to despair. I remember feeling 'this isn't working' but that time in the Volkswagen Beetle something happened. Why it didn't happen before, or at what point God actually did take me to be his child, I don't know, but I do know that from that point on I knew I was his. I can still remember the glorious feeling of knowing that I belonged to God.

In November 1961, a pastor was found for the Saltspring Island church so we moved to Regina, where we lived for the next five years. I remember breaking legs and arms, like most boys do. I was taught to swim by Louis Peskett who was Director of Youth for Christ in Edmonton at that time. Louis was killed on a mountain climbing expedition with a group of teenage lads off the streets of Edmonton. Years later I stood near the site of the accident in the middle of the Rockies as Canadian Government representatives named a mountain after Louis.

I was baptised in water when I was eight or nine. I remember crying when I came up out of the water and feeling the significance of the event; a year or so later I had an even more memorable spiritual experience.

An evangelist came to the town and for a month our church had three meetings a day to accommodate all who wanted to hear him. Every meeting was packed with hundreds of people. The morning meeting was for prayer; there was a teaching meeting in the afternoon and the evening meeting was a celebration time. We didn't get home until past midnight every night, though for a whole month we never missed one hour of school and were never tired. That was miraculous in itself. It really was a supernatural time and I haven't seen anything like it since. Though it started in the church, it spilled over into the city. There were all kinds of people getting converted off the streets; people who'd had no contact with church before that month. But at the same time there were death threats against my father. Some people came to the meeting and threatened Dad. For some reason a man phoned a death-threat to the church office before the evening service. The ushers and church deacons took it seriously. The church met in a long narrow building in a downtown area, with doors opening directly onto the street at one end with the pulpit directly opposite the doors at the other end of the building. Anyone with a good aim could open the door, take aim, fire at the pulpit and be gone before anyone could act. Careful measures were taken that evening and the service went off without a hitch; perhaps God intervened.

It was during that month that I first sensed God's call to be an evangelist. The call came in a dream. I dreamt I was in our back garden with a ladder beside me. I looked up and saw Jesus. It was as if he was hovering at the top of the ladder. I couldn't see his face because of the brilliance of the light around him. I felt incredibly peaceful as he spoke to me calling me to go into the whole world to preach the Gospel. I particularly remember that he said he would require me to take the Good News to distant lands. Then suddenly I felt I was soaring around the world with the clouds beneath me. No particular country was highlighted; there was just an impression of travel and going on his behalf. Suddenly, it was over.

I woke up abruptly and was terrified. I would describe it as the fear of God rather than a terror of a negative nature. I ran into my parents' room screaming, not hysterically but really upset because nothing like that had ever happened to me before. I knew it wasn't a dream in the normal sense. God had said something to me which has marked the whole of my life.

I woke up the next morning with the strong impression that I was eventually going to end up in Arab lands. Now I was studying Saudi Arabia in Geography at that point so it may have just been that, but that impression has lasted. I've never taken specific steps to make it happen, although I have been involved in work in the Sahara Desert through the Burkina Faso project – though that's many years down the line from this childhood dream. The point is that from that night on, although I was only ten years old, I knew I had been called to be an evangelist. Grandpa Sheppard's deathbed prayer was to be answered in my generation as well as my father's, although I am not the only one from my generation in full-time Christian work. (My brother Brent is a powerful and controversial communicator to young people; my sister Faith works in a large church in British Columbia and I have several cousins in full-time Christian work.)

My dream that night was deeply moving. I've rarely talked about it over the years as it was deeply personal to me, nor do I believe that it proves anything to anyone else, but I know that God called me to preach that night in February in the middle of a harsh Canadian winter.

5

A first conversion

In 1966 England won the World Cup, Billy Graham held the Greater London Crusade and The Beatles released 'Yellow Submarine'. The hippy movement was in full swing. We moved to Winnipeg that September and I remember the rioting as hippies challenged the authorities.

As I entered my teens I also began to challenge my parents' authority. I wanted to think through issues for myself; to decide what I thought about the sex, drugs and rock 'n' roll culture of my contemporaries. I wanted to choose my own clothes and grow my hair long. When Grandma Sheppard died in 1967 I went to the funeral but didn't cry. My sister accused me of being hard.

Life was certainly becoming tough for me in Winnipeg. The church was small and was in a rough area. I was beaten up from time to time by bullies who wanted to get at the 'preacher's kid'. My first paid job was delivering drugs for the drugstore (chemist shop). I had a white newspaper sack and would ride around on my bike on Monday and Wednesday evenings delivering tablets and medicines to customers. One night a gang of kids stole all the drugs and beat me up. As well as leaving my body battered and my pride dented, they left a growing resentment.

Being the 'preacher's kid' made me different from everyone else. I didn't have the things that other kids had. My clothes weren't quite as trendy and I always had what was called a 'brush cut'. My hair was so short I'd have been classed as a skin-head these days. My parents said 'When you grow your hair long, you rebel.' Certainly hair cuts always provoked heated arguments. I already felt abnormal. Short hair simply exaggerated the differences I felt.

Other youngsters in the area were part of 'normal' families and lived in 'normal' houses and had 'normal' lives. For us life was never the same from one year to the next. Even with the family, I felt different. Faith and Brent were both extroverts. Brent eventually went to a professional acting school and Faith directs her church's drama department. When we were children they loved to entertain the crowds of relatives and friends who crowded into our home on family occasions. I would sit out, partly because I felt inadequate; I still found speaking in public difficult; but also because, arrogantly, I thought a lot of what they did was frivolous. I'd rather sit in a corner and criticise.

Our constantly changing home life added to my feeling of being peculiar. Living in our own house was the exception rather than the rule as I grew up. We left the Winnipeg manse after two years because my father wanted to go back on the road as an itinerant evangelist. Even as my father's ministry became more established we lived on the road in a thirty-foot, luxury caravan – called an Air-Stream trailer – rather than staying in houses en route. It had television, air conditioning and was luxurious in many ways but it was cramped. There was a bedroom in the back where my parents slept. My brother and sister slept at the front on the settee that pulled out, and I slept on the floor in the middle. That's where I developed my habit of sleeping with earplugs to block out the noise of Dad snoring or Faith sniffing; to this day I can't sleep without the earplugs.

I felt deeply the lack of privacy. My sister and brother loved the lifestyle; Faith still loves the whole family being together in one place at one time. I didn't enjoy it at all because I didn't have any personal space. I only had a wardrobe to call my own. In my daydreams I would design a bedroom for myself with secret compartments where I could hide drugs.

Experimenting with drugs was one way in which I began to act out my rebellion. All my friends were trying different drugs. These weren't the kids at school, they were other church leaders' children. We were all rebelling against our parents' lifestyle, though I believe God protected me from taking anything which had a lasting impact. For example, on one occasion I'd ordered some marijuana, or grass as we called it, through a friend, but we left the area on another trip an hour before she arrived.

Although we were based in Winnipeg my father was out preaching every summer at Bible camps. I would get all fired up in the summer but then frightened to death to tell people I was a Christian when I got back to school. At the age of twelve I can remember quite distinctly travelling to the Trossachs Bible Camp, twenty miles from my grandfather's homestead, with my ear up against the rear speaker of one of these massive American cars, listening to rock 'n' roll music which my parents had banned. I had a discussion with myself as we went along: 'Will this summer be like every other summer where I get fired up and then I cool down when I get back to school?'

I hated the hypocrisy of that, and I knew I had a decision to make. Either I needed to be sold out to God or to give up and do what I wanted to do. My rationale was: 'I'm young, there are some things I want to do for myself, so although I know God's called me to work for him, I'm going to do what I want to do for a few years.'

It was a definite decision and, once I'd made it, I felt a physical sensation of darkness around me. That darkness marked my life for the next four years. With it came a sense of isolation and fear. I suppose this personal experience at the age of twelve has led to my strong commitment to reach people when they are young; adolescents make life-changing decisions.

I began to delve into the occult in a very mild way around that time. I heard about a chant you could recite so I tried with some of the other church leaders' kids in the church toilets of all places. I lived in terror of the dark, and even in a brightly lit room on my own I would often be gripped by a cold, clammy fear. My experience demonstrates the truth of Galatians chapter 5 where witchcraft is listed along with discord and dissension. I realise now that my rebellious decision had opened up a window for demonic influence. I still carry scars from that rebellious period. For example, although it's lessening all the time, I'm still afraid of the dark. I've prayed along with others and I've seen some improvement but I'm not totally healed yet. If Kande is away overnight I recite God's promise from 2 Corinthians 12:9 to get to sleep: 'My grace is sufficient for you, for my power is made perfect in weakness.' But I recite it with the corridor light on! Then I have a good sleep. My rebellion has had long term effects. I believe when God restores a person there are some instant changes that take place, but the damage of sin can linger and leave scars.

Early on in this very bleak period there was one highlight. I had my first experience of doing something for other people by taking part in the Miles for Millions Walk in Winnipeg. I joined forces with about 20,000 other people to walk 35 miles to raise money for poverty-stricken people in Haiti. I did it partly out of a sense of adventure; I wanted to do something different: my brother hadn't done anything like it; my sister hadn't and most of my school friends weren't doing it. I knew that I was a good runner, and I was confident that I could do it.

Although there was war in Vietnam, riots in Los Angeles, communist purges in China and the tragedy of the Biafran war breaking out in Nigeria, it was the first time I realised that there were needy people in the world.

The thought of poor and hungry people in Haiti mobilised me. To train for the walk, I tied bricks to the bottom of my training shoes, then ran up and down the lane behind our house. I must have looked ridiculous but I was determined; I took it very seriously as I wanted to do well, both because my pride was at stake and because it would raise the maximum amount for the people in Haiti.

Together with a friend, Doug Pearson, I walked 35 miles on the day. It took about 12 hours and was a great adventure; a real highlight of my childhood. Although I probably only raised a few pounds, I believed it was significant!

However, doing good for others didn't make a difference to my increasing rebelliousness at home. My father says the four years before my sixteenth birthday were one long argument. My relationship with my mother completely disintegrated during those years.

When I was fourteen we came to England for one year and I continued my schooling by correspondence. I detested Britain and pined for the Rocky Mountains and Canadian cedar forests. Britain, with its brick buildings and densely populated cities, felt over-crowded and polluted. You couldn't get away from people, noise and dirt. I celebrated my fifteenth birthday at Stratford-upon-Avon. There were power cuts that year and the Conservatives won a General Election. But I wasn't interested in politics or in anything British. I just felt the cold. My sister counted the different beds we slept in on our travels that year; they came to 65 in all!

A Canadian businessman had paid all our airfares for a mission tour among the Assemblies of God and Elim Pentecostal churches. While we were touring Britain holding mission meetings my father gave me the responsibility of the book table at the back of the halls where we met. That's where my interest in financial affairs began. I was allowed to have a percentage of everything I sold. It was only pennies of course but for a 14-year-old with no other source of income it was a great incentive. As well as making some money for myself I went into business producing souvenir pens with 'Sheppard Family' and our Canadian address stamped on them. I would enthusiastically count the takings each night after the meeting. Although I was an angry and a rebellious adolescent I still had a softness for my father's ministry. I didn't want to ruin it and wanted him to succeed. I even prayed during his appeals that people would respond.

Despite my hardness God seemed to be planting ideas for future ministry. In my day dreams I devised an evangelistic organisation, and I went into fine detail designing the premises we would need, the size of the team, the drama and music we would use. It's as if God was planting things for the future. I drew up budgets and job descriptions just for fun; rather than spend time on my school work I'd spend hours drafting my plans. About that time I read the book of Proverbs and I can still sense the hunger that I felt then for the wisdom that Proverbs talks about. This prompted me to read more widely as I began to see that faith touches every part of our society. This seems strange with hindsight as, at the time, I was intensely hostile to God and his will for me.

It must have been very difficult for my parents during these years. Although I went along with them, and even read my Bible and prayed from time to time, I was constantly challenging their authority. I threatened to hit my mother several times when she tried to reprimand or discipline me. It was as if I had no love for her at all. They wanted me to be part of the family; the whole family played a part in the missions Dad led and usually sat on the platform with him, so it was a bit embarrassing if I wasn't there. They contemplated sending me away to a private school or quitting the ministry themselves. They were at their wits' end as my father knew that the Bible clearly stated: 'An elder must be blameless, the husband of but one wife, a man whose children believe and are not open to the charge of being wild or disobedient' (Titus 1:6). He was debating whether he was qualified to continue in ministry. It was not that anyone else was pointing an accusing finger but they struggled with the scriptural principle.

Once we returned home to Canada I gravitated towards other rebels. I never had the chance to go out on the streets and be with the real hippies of that day, but there were plenty of other rebels in the church. I never once got drunk and I never got stoned on drugs, but it wasn't for want of trying. Perhaps God in his sovereignty was keeping me safe from myself.

I didn't want to do chemical drugs like LSD, but even at the Bible camps we went to I mixed with the guys who were dealing in drugs. For example, one summer, Glen and Kelly, my two friends who were both dealing in 'Acid,' got hold of some 18-hour pills. Up to then they'd had pills which gave a 6–8 hour 'high'. They decided to take the 18-hour pills at camp where there were people to help them. They each dropped a tablet and said they'd never enjoyed church so much as that particular evening! Because I didn't take the tablets I had the job of being their minder. I remember pretending to pull their noses off and throw them into the lake. At two o'clock in the morning they were running into the lake to retrieve a piece of their face!

The only Christians who made any impression on me were the 'Jesus People'. This was the name given by the North American media to the growing number of hippies who were being converted on the streets. There was something genuine and attractive about these groups and 'Jesus People' churches were springing up all over the States and Canada. One church we visited in Arizona had only been started the year before but there were three hundred hippies attending. Even there, however, after I'd sung with the family on the platform, I'd sneak off outside and do all kinds of things in the car park. One day I was followed out by a hippie who looked like a grizzly bear, over six feet tall with long hair down to his waist. He wrapped his arms around me, knowing what kind of a rascal I was, and just said how much he loved me and that

God loved me. The Jesus I saw in those hippies attracted me . . . it began to soften me.

The crunch came at Mooselake Camp in northern Alberta in 1971 where my dad was the preacher. Up to that point I'd always thought that I would come back to God at some point. Halfway through the week, together with a friend called Hughie Marks, I broke the camp rules by canoeing across the lake and staying out too late. We discovered two girls from California with their own ski-boat and we skied with them for the whole afternoon. We weren't back at camp by the curfew time. Pentecostal camps in Canada were very strict. I was the evangelist's son and was expected to be a good example.

When I did return my father was very angry and I was in a rage. Dad was controlling himself, but in his anger he said, 'You're going to ruin my ministry.'

I didn't need to hear that, so I walked out of the caravan, slamming the door shut saying: 'God, that's it. I thought I might come back to you sometime, but I don't want this for my life. This is it, I'm never going to come back to you.'

I went to the evening meeting as usual and sat at the front; remember all this time I'm still an evangelist's son and I'm still singing with the family on stage while ordering marijuana from my friends. I did what was required of me mechanically, then left to do my own thing.

That night I sat there as my father preached about the Cross. It was a message I'd heard many times before; I'd heard all the illustrations. But suddenly I had a revelation of my darkness and a fresh understanding of the fact that Christ died for me. It was a classic case of conviction of sin and a revelation of truth. And I just gave in to it. I couldn't ignore the profound truth that Jesus loves me!!! It breaks your heart and you can't run away from that kind of love once it's been made known to you. I'd known it in my head but, somehow it had sunk down to my heart.

Everyone's conversion experience is different. Mine was highly emotional. Tears flowed and I had a wonderful feeling of cleansing and stepping into light from darkness; there's no better description of it.

The first sign of my conversion was reconciliation with my mother. We'd lived in the same caravan; she made my meals and she washed my clothes, but I hated her. I know that's a very strong word and the hate was undeserved, but it was my spiritual condition that caused it. She stood for everything I didn't want and so I hated her.

As I looked across at the other side of the large log chapel where the evening meeting was being held, I could see my mother in a distant corner sitting looking at me. Immediately I knew that she was enjoying every moment of seeing me come back to God. At the same time I knew she did not want to come to me because of my feelings towards her. She didn't want anything to stop what was happening to me. As soon as I saw her, love welled up inside me and I moved towards her. We cried; I apologised and our relationship was restored. It was wonderful, so wonderful that I was afraid to go to bed that night in case the feelings wouldn't be there any more. My mother wisely said that the work God does is a permanent work and even if the feelings disappeared I'd have confidence that God had worked in my life. The great feelings were still there the next day, and for the rest of the week, even when I was water-skiing it kept hitting me: 'I'm clean!'

My parents were thrilled, but on the last day of the camp something happened to make them think it had all been a sham. My father and the camp manager came to make sure we had cleaned out our cabin. Beside my bunk bed there was a shelf and on it they found a capsule about two inches long that said LSD on it in big bold letters. They went into quite a state, using two sticks to lift it because they didn't want to touch it. They brought it into the dining room; we were all summoned and challenged about the dangers of leading a double life. Of course my father was deeply disappointed to think that his son hadn't made any recovery at all from his backslidden state.

We all arrived wondering what was happening, then we

saw the capsule on the table. The drummer from the band went over and opened it up and pulled out the Gospel tract that was inside, much to the relief of the camp manager and especially my father! God had changed me and this time there would be no going back.

6

Changes

My changed relationship with God started a series of other changes in my life. The reconciliation with my mother had to be worked out on a day to day level. I had been angry with God and the world and had expressed that anger most fiercely towards her. As a result of my fresh encounter with God at the camp, the anger gave way to love. Of course we still had arguments, but the hatred wasn't there; heated debates were underscored with love.

My reading habits began to change as my appetite for truth began to grow. As I read the works of Francis Schaeffer and C.S. Lewis I realised, for the first time, that faith touches every part of our lives and society. When my world view changed it was as if I was looking at everything with a different pair of eyes. I'd had glimpses before, but from then on the world looked different. I still had to grow up emotionally and psychologically; there were lots of things I had to learn, but my state of mind had changed.

My attitude to other people changed too. While I was running away from God I'd become self-absorbed. I desperately wanted to be liked and everything I did was motivated by that desire to be accepted by other people, rather than to obey God. I was convinced that if I was a Christian I wouldn't be liked at school. After the camp I was still frightened as to how I would relate my faith to school life. The school was in an upper middle-class area, so there was a lot of money available to buy drugs. I didn't do very well that year in declaring my Christian faith, but being back with God did mean I stayed out of the drug scene. It wasn't until we moved to San Antonio in Texas, and I was in my final year at High School, that I became more open as a Christian.

No adolescent's story would be complete without some struggles relating to boy – girl relationships and my teenage years were not without testing and learning on that score. Being a 'preacher's kid' still made me feel different from everyone else even after I was reconciled to God and my parents. My less fashionable clothes, brush-cut and travelling life-style, marked me out. And, at a time when most teenagers are breaking loose from parental rule, I was still living in a caravan. Even in Texas, when my parents were given a two-bedroomed bungalow on campus, my parents and brother slept in the house while my sister slept in the girls' dormitory and I slept in a small caravan in the drive. I longed for a 'normal' lifestyle.

To add to all that, I had a speech impediment, so I always felt inferior. The impediment worsened when girls were around; I'd just freeze. From the age of about twelve when my friends began to ask girls out, I'd be left struggling along behind. I wasn't able to relate to girls and, when finally I did make friends with a girl, I took it all too seriously.

I was only about seventeen at the time and Cindy was about a year and a half older than me. She was the Camp Director's daughter during a Bible camp we took part in as a family. We arrived early for the camp, and as she was the only other young person there, we spent a lot of time together. Our first kiss was a major hurdle and the most embarrassing moment of my life as I missed! But romance blossomed in spite of my clumsiness.

As she was an excellent singer, my father asked her parents if she could travel with us for the whole summer singing at the Bible camps in which my family was involved. Our friendship went from strength to strength in those six weeks and, by the time we got to Ontario, we were already talking about marriage. Although my family moved to Texas straight after that summer, Cindy and I wrote to each other almost daily for about nine months.

She was considering becoming a nurse, so I got hold of nursing books to help me write letters that were relevant to her. I flew up to visit her at Christmas and, although we had a few disagreements, I didn't really see the age gap. Looking back now I must have been much less mature than her and must have been much more infatuated with her than she was with me. But we kept writing and she came to Texas for Easter. I thought everything was going well until summer came and she broke off the relationship. I might have coped well enough, but it wasn't a clean break. I pestered her several times to get back together over the summer. The on/off relationship hurt both of us. She finally broke it off for good.

However, my time in Texas was not without its more positive lessons. I wanted to be open about my faith and, once we reached Texas and a new set of friends, I was determined to demonstrate I was a Christian right from the start. One example of this new openness was a Halloween outreach. My friend and I took a pile of tracts explaining the dangers of Halloween and put them under the wiper blades on cars in local shopping malls. Looking back, it was probably a waste of paper, but it showed that we wanted to do something active to show our faith.

Living as a Christian from day to day was more difficult, but I'm sure it was infinitely more effective. From the start of my time in Texas I wanted my classmates to get to know Jesus too. I thought the best way was to take my Bible to school. So from day one I carried my Bible with me. At the beginning of the year it was at the bottom of my stack of books, but by the end I carried it at the top; an insignificant change, perhaps, but it demonstrated my changing priorities.

All my life I had wanted to be liked by people and I'd thought that wearing the Christian label would mean I'd be rejected. But that year at school I was more popular than I'd ever been before. People called me 'The Bishop', but in a friendly warm way rather than to be hostile or malicious. Being a Canadian in Texas made me a bit of a novelty; they thought all Canadians were Eskimos; so when it came to the end of the year they threw a farewell party for me. That made me realise I'd been wrong; it was possible to be known as a Christian and be respected as well. I thought 'God, I've wasted so many years. I should have done this back in grade five. My life would have been a whole lot easier!' It was an important lesson.

Learning to live my Christian life in public was one thing; developing that faith privately was another. After leaving school I spent a year at Bible College in Saskatchewan and was embarrassed to discover that I didn't even know all the books in the Bible existed. I knew the Gospel and other key subjects, like tithing, which my father had preached on, but I didn't have a wide understanding of Scripture. If I had, I might have realised that the Bible held the answers to the questions I was asking in life. I had never read the Bible regularly and, even when I had a faith of my own, I had my ups and downs in terms of daily Bible reading. I didn't like the legalism of a Bible reading ritual, but I recognised my need for spiritual food. At times since then I've gone through periods when I've read twenty chapters a day for months on end, reading right through the Bible several times. At other times I've read only a few verses a day or none at all. But what I had from the age of sixteen was a hunger to know God, though it took a while to realise that I could discover God through Scripture.

Having made the break with Cindy, I was annoyed with life generally. I fitted right into a year when rebellion was bubbling just below the surface. The college dean said it was the worst year he'd ever had. We were wild and broke all the rules. Although we didn't get drunk, we had alcohol on the premises; girls were in boys' dorms for all-night parties and, although nothing immoral went on, we broke every rule in the book. I threw myself into it as a way to forget Cindy. I had a thoroughly good time, but failed every course.

After one year at Bible college I went back to Vancouver where I enrolled in a part-time Bible college course and worked for a carpenter in the afternoons and evenings. Spiritually I was going through a cold patch and, although I tried to take the college course seriously, I had still not recovered from the hurts of that first teenage romance. I went from one short relationship to another and refused to submit to God's direction for my life. I was more interested in making money and mapping out my own life. When I landed a job as an advertising salesman on a newspaper, I jumped at the chance and condensed the last few weeks of the Bible college course to finish early.

The job was with a weekly paper and, although I was mainly involved in advertisement sales, I did a bit of writing and photography as well. It was during that period that God began to put the screws on me through things people said and through issues that came up in the church meetings I attended. I spent a lot of time driving through the countryside on ad-sales jobs, praying and taking stock of life. Gradually I began to realise that God wanted me to preach. As this conviction grew I began to develop grand evangelistic strategies, though the balance between pure fun and effective communication was questionable.

Work went well and I met the targets; in fact if I hadn't been involved in church life I might have made quite a good ad salesman. But as long as I kept the bosses satisfied I preferred to concentrate my efforts on other things. Life wasn't all church but most of life's experiences became food for youth group or mission strategies. When I was chosen to represent the newspaper in a car race at a local track, I came in second and was so excited about my new-found talent that I imagined organising a Christian cross-country car rally with co-drivers throwing Bibles out of the car windows as they zoomed through remote villages. My mind was always full of ideas for evangelism, no matter how stupid they may have been!

During that time I also took flying lessons. I was gradually recognising that God had plans for my life and, as I thought and prayed about what He might want me to do, it seemed like he was pointing me to Mexico. I'd been to Mexico with my family years before and I hadn't liked it at all. I didn't like the dirt, the corruption or the lifestyle; in fact the only aspect of Mexican life that attracted me was the work of a missionary we'd met there. John Eils was a pilot with his own plane to take him into jungle regions as he spread the Gospel. That appealed to my sense of adventure, so I took up flying and made a deal with God saying: 'Okay, I've two weeks holiday coming up. If John Eils will accept me, I'll spend the time in Mexico. But if you really want me to go to Mexico for longer you'll have to get rid of my dislike for the place.'

I made all the arrangements and flew to Mexico City that autumn on an Air Mexico plane which had water leaking through the roof when it flew at low levels; I expected the rubber band to break at any minute! I was met at the airport by John Eils and was thrown into two wonderful weeks packed with adventure.

My first encounter with rural Mexico has left lasting impressions. I'd only been in Mexico for a couple of days when John flew me and another missionary, Sam Cooksey, out to a remote village. Then Sam and I walked about five miles into the bush to an even more isolated village where Sam was planning to bring an evangelistic film. It was easy to buy a bottle of Coca Cola in this inaccessible place – it gets world-wide distribution – but for the first time in my life I met someone who had never heard of Jesus.

Pedro was about sixteen and, as we sat talking in one of the village shacks, he bombarded us with questions. Although he followed Roman Catholic traditions like the rest of his village, and he had lots of friends called Jesus, he had no idea that Jesus Christ was a historical person.

He certainly didn't know that this Jesus had died for him. Meeting Pedro had a profound effect on me. I cried that night for all the people God had created, who didn't even know He loved them. Suddenly my distaste for Mexico turned to love and that night I said: 'Okay, I will come to Mexico.'

During the rest of my stay I talked to John about the possibility of joining his team as an apprentice in all areas of the work, but particularly on the aviation side as a student pilot. He said I could join the following spring, so I returned home to talk with my parents and our church leaders about my first steps as a missionary. The church had just started an apprentice missionary programme to provide funds for young people taking part in mission work for up to one year. The theory was that if they could hack it for a year, they'd go back full time. Our church was a great missionary-sending church and had more than a dozen experienced missionaries around the world. They hadn't taken risks with young people before and I was the first one to be accepted for the scheme. Fortunately it all worked out very smoothly. With the backing of the church and my parents, I handed in my resignation to the newspaper and began to finalise arrangements for the move to Mexico. A new phase of life and adventure was about to begin.

7

Tasting adventure and adversity

In February 1976 I went to Mexico, visiting friends on the way. It was the year that Jimmy Carter won the American Presidential election, James Callaghan took over from Harold Wilson as the British Prime Minister and the Chinese leader Mao Tse-tung died; Concorde flew from Europe to America for the first time and Viking I sent back the first detailed pictures from Mars. I was 21 and felt that a new world was opening up for me. I was a missionary on my way to fly planes for God and I was sure it was going to be great fun. However, my adventures got off to a bad start. I stayed with a friend whose marriage broke up right at the time I was with him.

The experience forced me to recognise the mess people can make of their lives and the pain that they live with when they break out of God's guidelines for living. I was shattered because my friend was a man I had admired. My own mother and father's marriage was so strong; Dad would avoid anything with even a suggestion of evil, so broken marriages and immorality were completely new to me.

As a result of the experience I arrived in Mexico slightly more aware of the real world, but my adventuring, idealised view of missionary life was still intact. Apart from a bag of belongings, I proudly carried a hunting bow; I had romantic dreams of killing wild hog in Mexico for food! Instead of facing ferocious beasts in the jungle I encountered more practical difficulties. I faced the dilemma of getting past customs officers who were in the habit of receiving bribes from foreigners who wanted an uninterrupted journey; the more you paid the faster you were processed!

The ordeal brought me face to face with the corruption that I'd seen and hated on my first trip to Mexico. People lived in fear of the authorities. It was such a contrast to America and Canada where corruption is usually hidden behind the cloak of respectability. In Mexico there were teenage prostitutes on the streets with adolescent pimps saying: 'Hey mister, do you want to buy my sister?' Drugs were sold freely on street corners and trumped-up charges were part of the way of life. I was glad to reach the safety of John Eils' farm and the Christian community which was so wholesome in contrast to its surroundings.

John Eils was full of life; a man in his forties who loved having fun. His blond hair and blue eyes made him look Scandinavian; his beaming smile and large frame meant his presence was always noticed and appreciated. As he only slept for four or five hours a night, when we'd meet for breakfast at about 7am he would have already swum five kilometres in the local pool or had a game of tennis. If we'd been out flying all day, or showing a film in some remote village not getting back until after midnight, John would still want to play chess or some board game. When asked why he didn't sleep more, his response was always the same: 'Why sleep your life away, when you don't know how long it's going to be?' It was as if he had a sense that he was going to die young. Josie, his wife, refused to fly with him in case they both died in an accident. Sadly, only two years after I left Mexico, he was killed in an air crash, fulfilling every premonition that he and others seemed to have had.

John enjoyed life to the full and everyone else gravitated

towards him because of that. I wouldn't say he was the best preacher in the world, but when he got behind the pulpit people hung on every word. He was a gifted storyteller and had a fund of hair-raising experiences to keep listeners amused. He'd been arrested once for allegedly running a brothel; that story prompted the title of his biography 'The Scandalous Saint'; and although Bible schools were illegal in Mexico, he opened one, but called it 'The Nest of Eagles' to avoid legal restrictions.

Since he'd arrived in Mexico he'd established a farm, north of Victoria, an orphanage to the south and the Bible college. Honey and other produce from the farm funded the Bible college and kept the orphanage going. A Texan called Ercel Lewis ran the farm and, like John, he was lots of fun to be with. Whenever we went up to the farm he'd arrange a rodeo with cows instead of horses. We'd climb onto these cows to see who could stay on the longest, then Ercel would kick them so that they'd rear up and try to throw us off. It was a friendly, healthy community lifestyle. We played together as well as working together and, although there were tensions and arguments, they were worked through. I learned a lot by watching how they dealt with difficulties and conflicts.

At the start of my stay I was assigned a tutor to learn Spanish; he was one of the team at the orphanage who was my age. Unfortunately we didn't get on at all. He was very right-wing and pro-American which rubbed me up the wrong way, so I didn't do well in my language lessons. I mastered some Spanish from him and tried to learn on my own from a book, but the missionaries quickly became aware that I wasn't student material, so they decided to try a different approach.

One of John Eils' practical jokes was the catalyst to my language studies. We were at the breakfast table one morning when he announced that they were going to teach me a Spanish phrase every morning at breakfast and I was to use it throughout the day. To start they were going to teach me how to tell a waitress I was ready to order my meal. They told me to say: 'Yo quero besarte.' So I practised it several times in their presence and got the pronunciation fairly good. Then when the waitress came to the table I threw my shoulders back and with a silly grin on my face, full of confidence, I said: 'Yo quero besarte.' Immediately she giggled and looked embarrassed. I thought it was because of my accent but I persevered for weeks using the phrase every time I ordered a meal from a waitress or waiter. Each time I got the same reaction, except once a waiter winked at me when I said my piece.

After six weeks a waitress who served me could also speak English and when I came out with my three words she asked, 'Do you know what you're saying?'

I said, 'Of course, I'm telling you I'm ready to order my meal.'

To my horror she replied, 'No you're not, you're telling me you want to kiss me. ''I want to kiss you'' is the literal translation!'

Well, I went home and studied Spanish for about twelve hours straight off that day, embarrassed that I had been a joke for so long among all the missionaries. They had taught me a very important lesson.

It was about that time that I became convinced that God was calling me to England, not because I couldn't face learning a new language, nor for any emotional reasons. It simply became obvious; as if God was saying: 'Go to England, young man, go to England.' With the initial idea came a growing confidence that England would be where I'd end up. I had disliked Britain when I'd visited it as a teenager and I didn't know when or how I'd be going back, but I was convinced that God was preparing me for England.

Part of the preparation which complemented my time in Mexico was a Bible smuggling trip to Cuba. I went with a friend called Terry Small, a school teacher from my church in Vancouver. He had joined me for a ten-day holiday in Mexico and together we acted as couriers for a Bible smuggling organisation. Americans were not allowed to travel to Cuba, but two Canadians flying in from Mexico were ideal couriers. As well as Bibles, we took a variety of other goods to help Cuban Christians, from false teeth to car parts. Cuban Christians were registered by the government and weren't allowed access to some of the things that other Cubans enjoyed, although everybody was on rations. Every item we took was designated for a particular Christian in response to a church leader's request. It wasn't real smuggling because everything in our suitcases could be seen if a customs officer took more than a cursory look. The only things that were partly concealed were the car parts that I carried in the inside pockets of my jacket, but even then a frisk would have revealed those.

When we flew into Havana we landed about midnight. At three o'clock in the morning, Terry and I were still there, the last passengers in the customs room. The officers had all of our goods laid across the table, including 500 pieces of Christian literature. When they asked me why I was bringing such a quantity of literature into Cuba I didn't know what to say, but blurted out, 'I read a lot!' It seemed to satisfy them, and they let us go.

Our movements were all very covert after that. We had to meet people in back lanes and use code names on the telephone. But we were probably more paranoid than we needed to be. One night I even took the coded directions we had been given and flushed them down the loo. We hadn't been instructed to do that but Terry and I had seen one too many spy films and it seemed like a good idea!

Being on our own was frightening and we didn't really have much fun in Havana. But it gave me a glimpse of what it is like to be a Christian under persecution; where you have to register that you are a Christian even though it means you won't get a university education or a good job. Churches were not allowed to repair their buildings, and ministers were considered to have a lower profession than that of a prostitute. But in spite of that kind of pressure we saw joy, unity and perseverance in the Christians we met, alongside all the suffering. It gave flesh and bones to the Bible's teaching, that 'the gates of hell shall not prevail' against the Church.

It was in the Cuban context of persecution that I heard eye-witness accounts of miracles. One pastor had a 1951 Chevrolet. New cars weren't available after the Cuban revolution, especially not for Christians, so this man kept on using this Chevrolet to pick up senior citizens to take them to church. It had worked right up to the end of the sixties when a Christian mechanic flew in from Mexico City to try to repair it. He took one look at it and pronounced it dead; there was nothing he could do to get the car started.

Undaunted, the pastor got the elders of the church together, anointed the car with oil and prayed for it. I've no idea what kind of oil it was, but when the pastor got into the car after they had prayed he simply turned the ignition and it started perfectly. For the next two years all they had to replace was petrol. Shortly before I arrived soldiers had tried to confiscate the car but when they turned the ignition nothing happened. After that the church nicknamed the car 'Lazarus'.

The Lazarus episode and other accounts of miracles, began to teach me that necessity is the mother of faith. You are forced to rely on God when you have no other options. The lesson came home most forcibly to us when we set off for Santa Clara, the heart of Fidel Castro's revolution. We didn't have the necessary authorisation to go there – you had to have your passports stamped with permission to travel from one province to another – but the family we were to visit had risked everything to stay there. We had brought some goods into the country for people in the area and we were keen to meet a couple of Canadian missionaries who ran a Bible college just outside Santa Clara. Even after the revolution they had stayed on because they knew that if they ever left their land it would be confiscated. They hadn't been home to see their family in Canada for about twenty years. We went to visit them, but the only contact we had was the name of the minister in Santa Clara itself. We weren't exactly sure where we were heading.

When we got to the bus depot in Havana, we waited hours for a bus. Finally someone came and tapped on my shoulder and pointed us in the right direction. It was a nightmarish trip through the dark tropical night. Chickens and other animals were crammed on board with all the passengers. I was really frightened and felt deeply depressed. This was no stirring escapade for two fearless adventurers; we had no reservoirs of faith surging up to assure us that God was with us and all would be well. We were leaving Havana with its airport and route back to freedom and were surrounded by people we could hardly understand, heading for Fidel Castro's stronghold, with the name of one man as our only source of help. Suddenly Santa Clara was no longer a little dot on the map, but a big city!

When we got off the bus there was a queue for taxis so we joined it not knowing what else to do. We didn't know what we would say to the driver when we reached the head of the queue. There were probably at least fifty people in front of us. We talked in whispers, trying to decide our course of action, and probably looked very nervous and suspicious. Suddenly the lady in front of us turned round and said, in broken English, 'Are you Christians?'

In a totalitarian state, when you're some place that you shouldn't be and you're a Christian, you are reluctant to announce the fact to a stranger. But at the same time, not being able to lie, we conceded that we were. She immediately replied, 'Well I'm a Christian too.'

We were overwhelmed with relief and, when she asked where we were going, we showed her this little piece of paper with the pastor's name on it and discovered to our amazement that she was also going to visit him. It was a miracle! Suddenly I realised God was with us after all; he had put the lady ahead of us in the queue. Our faith took a giant leap forward at that point because it was more than coincidence; it was a God-arranged meeting.

She took us to see the minister and the next day he took us out to the Canadians' farm. It was such a challenge to our Christian commitment to see this aged couple, cut off from their family, but persevering under all the restraints of Castro's regime. They were still preaching the Gospel although they constantly risked losing their liberty and property.

The experience planted seeds in my heart and mind about the value of suffering. In the same way that the believers in Acts embraced persecution and saw God working miracles or multiplying their evangelistic efforts, the Christians we met in Cuba were seeing God at work in a more practical and yet supernatural way than I ever did in comfortable, affluent Canada. Although we were eager to return to the freedom of Mexico, the experience marked a significant step in my understanding of the adventure God has planned for those willing to trust Him.

Leaving Cuba was not as easy as we hoped. We were so eager to return to Mexico that we arrived at the airport ten hours early. We checked in, got our boarding passes and passports stamped and went to sit in the waiting room. An hour before we were due to fly an announcement came over the loudspeaker calling me back to the customs office. When we'd arrived in the country they had catalogued the contents of my bags which were now empty apart from a few personal belongings; the officers wanted to know why. You can imagine the shock I felt. To make matters worse Terry disowned me and walked off in the opposite direction! He told me later that he thought that if both of us were arrested there would be no way of raising prayer support back in Canada. Who would lobby for our release? We joke about it together now: he says he was assuming the awful responsibility of alerting my family, allowing me the privilege of being imprisoned!

We were both convinced that I was doomed to spend the next twenty years in a Cuban prison. They did want to know why I had two empty suitcases rather than four full ones, but they were curious rather than aggressive in their inquiry. Without having to lie, I was able to satisfy them by saying I had met some friends and had given my belongings away. I didn't tell them that it was an organised network with pre-arranged depots to deliver specifically requested goods. We had been trained to answer truthfully, but only to answer the specific questions that we were asked. It was certainly true to say that the people I had given things to had become my friends, but I was extremely relieved to board the plane. The ten-day trip had been traumatic at times, but it had forced me to face the shallowness of my faith in contrast to the Cuban Christians' depth of faith which had been forged in the crucible of persecution.

Back in Mexico I reflected a lot on my first experience of Communism. I had leftist sympathies, partly out of rebellion and partly as a reaction to the injustice of poverty. But I recognised there was injustice under Communism as well as Capitalism. People in Cuba had been robbed of the incentive to change their lives and robbed of their liberty to do so. They were not free to develop their own businesses or choose their own path in life. Human resources were being wasted. There was not the squalor or homelessness that can be found in some otherwise affluent inner-cities; basic shelter and medical care was provided by the state and, although food was rationed, people didn't go hungry. But there were queues for everything, unless you happened to be members of the ruling elite.

In contrast, soon after I returned to Mexico I experienced a taste of a completely different standard of living. I had become friends with a wealthy family who were members of a church in Mexico City. The daughter, Martha, was training to be an opera singer and we struck up a friendship. Martha's uncle had been the President of Mexico, but her immediate family had all become Christians and were trying to use their wealth to provide low-cost housing for poverty-stricken Mexicans. It was quite a novelty for me, a middle-class Canadian preacher's son, to mix with the Mexican aristocracy.

Not long after I returned from Cuba I came down with

typhoid. I was staying at a missionary's house at the time, not far from Martha's family home. When she came to visit she found me in a delirious state and phoned her dad to arrange for a driver to pick me up so her family could care for me. I am still grateful for their kindness, but also reminded of the contrast of lifestyle between the rich and the poor.

Spending time with her family gave me an insight into a different world; the world of wealth and ease which a tiny percentage of Mexicans enjoy, surrounded by the overwhelming poverty of the majority. Martha's family were trying to use their wealth wisely; I can only imagine what they would have been like before they were Christians.

I left Mexico in September 1976 as there was growing political unrest and talk of revolution. Expatriates were being advised to leave until the unrest, surrounding the change of president, subsided. Most of John Eils' team moved north over the border and waited. As it was getting close to Christmas, and there was no apparent change in the Mexican situation, I decided to return home. It was January before the political situation cooled and the team could return to their work. As I was supposed to complete my year with John Eils in February, I did not go back.

Although I had gone to Mexico with missionary aspirations, the most significant changes that took place as a result were in me and not in the people I met. Most of my contact with Mexicans was from a plane dropping leaflets or from behind a projector as we showed an evangelistic film. I never mastered the language and never identified fully with the people. But I changed in Mexico. I began to discover that the real adventure of faith is not hacking through remote jungles or piloting planes in faraway places, but living with the daily grind of persecution or poverty and seeing them transformed by a supernatural God. I thought I was an intrepid adventurer, but when I met God's genuine adventurers my fear of persecution and love of security stood out in sharp contrast to their risky, fearless living cocooned only by God's hands. By stripping me of my romantic view of missionary life God was preparing me for adventures which I could not have planned or dreamed.

8

A second conversion

The experiences of Cuba and Mexico provoked much thought. As I look back over developments in the Christian faith in Latin America since then, I realise that I was not the only one to catch a glimpse of God's heartbeat for that developing continent. The issue of liberation theology has, since then, become controversial. At the time it was embryonic. I was unable to articulate the issue in the terms used by many Roman Catholic activists and theologians, but I felt something of the concern they felt. I saw and was repulsed by the oppression, the corruption and the ordinary people's powerlessness, both in the communist regime of Cuba and the right-wing dictatorship in Mexico. I began to feel compassion for people who had no hope and could not even dream of advancement. Years later Bob Pierce, founder of World Vision International, the world's largest Christian aid organisation, told me that to be a man of God, you must feel what is breaking God's heart and allow it to break your heart as well. That heart-breaking process began in Mexico where I cried genuine, unselfish tears for the first time as I saw the plight of the people.

Liberation theology has been shaped significantly by Roman Catholic workers in Latin America attempting to make theology relevant to poverty and powerlessness.

While not agreeing with all of its assumptions or conclusions, theology or methodology, I am challenged by it because it has roots in the human heart and seeks freedom. It is a theme that runs through history from the children of Israel escaping Egypt through to African slaves crying out for freedom from their masters' oppression. Liberation theology remains unpopular with those in power and makes many Christians uncomfortable as it challenges middle class satisfaction with the status quo.

Poverty, oppression and powerlessness are the starting point of liberation theology. It attempts to make theology practical and relevant. Instead of asking 'Where is the God of truth in a world of science and technology?' it asks 'Where is the God of righteousness in a world of poverty?' Although Latin America has produced the most developed theologies of liberation, it is evident elsewhere, particularly in South Africa, though also in Europe (see Andrew Kirk's *Theology Encounters Revolution* (IVP)). In Britain this resurgence of interest in social action can be seen among evangelicals who are keen to care for the whole person; body and spirit.

One of the key liberation theologians, Brazilian priest Leonardo Boff, describes liberation theology as 'a kind of chemical reaction: faith plus oppression equals liberation theology'. Of course, some have accused liberation theologians of being Marxist in origin and conclusion. I don't adhere to all aspects of this theology, but it challenges me, particularly as I have seen for myself the poverty and oppression in South America which prompted its development.

We need to understand that truth is truth, whether it is an ass that speaks or a man, whether it is a preacher or Karl Marx; truth is truth. Jesus said the truth would come and set people free. The whole of Scripture is about liberation and we must not let our paranoia about other ideologies rob us of God's truth and his compassion for the world.

Liberation theology is about action rather than academic

study. We must take care in applying it because of its emphasis on political and social salvation which can undermine the supernatural elements of the Christian faith. Some liberation theologians view the world in Marxist terms as a class struggle which denies the existence of spiritual warfare between God and the kingdom of darkness. By recognising the structural sin to which liberation theologians point, we must not overlook the sinfulness of personal rebellion and the need for personal repentance.

The Lausanne Covenant of 1974 states, 'The message of salvation implies also the message of judgement on every form of alienation, oppression and discrimination and we should not be afraid to denounce evil and injustice wherever they exist.'

Oscar Romero, the Archbishop of San Salvador who was assassinated when leaving his pulpit, seemed to hold a balance by saying: 'Let us not put our trust in earthly liberation movements; yes they are providential, but only if they do not forget that all the liberating force in the world comes from Christ.'

Romero was aware of the spiritual forces at work and the dynamic of light entering darkness when he said, 'A preaching that awakens, a preaching that enlightens, as when a light turned on awakens a noisy sleeper; that is the preaching of Christ calling "Wake up, be converted". That is the Church's authentic preaching. Naturally, such preaching must meet conflict, must spoil what is mis-called "prestige", must disturb, must be persecuted. It cannot get along with the powers of darkness and sin.'

Going back to what happened to me in South America, I found that for the first time my emotions were opened up to the heartbeat of God. There is no doubt that there is a bias to the poor in Scripture and, although the Gospel is for everyone, it definitely does defend the cause of those who are on the outside. Jesus' inaugural message says it all: 'I have come to bring Good News to the poor.'

I believe that authentic Christianity affects the emotions

as well as the mind. I heard a friend say once that there is nothing more attractive than a truly-redeemed person in touch with the sensual world: someone who is connected with his or her feelings, who knows how to cry and how to laugh at the appropriate times. We need to take a lead from Jesus who cried tears of anguish and, from the Cross, a cry of abandonment to God: 'Why have you forsaken me?' As he was hanging on the Cross, Jesus felt and saw all the pain, oppression and powerlessness of humans throughout history. He felt the humiliation of the beggar, the confusion of the abused, the torn heart of the divorced, the imprisonment of poverty, the fear of powerlessness, the captivity of the prisoner, the terror of the battered wife, the numbness of the oppressed, the grief of the bereaved, the loneliness of the homeless and the pressure of the persecuted; he felt it all. He was no cool, calculating, passive bystander, offering only a strategy for salvation. He was and is the Christ who walked the path of suffering and pain, leading the way to salvation through the Cross. That is why I believe that Jesus always hears the cries of those who are experiencing authentic pain and powerlessness.

Years ago in my youth group in Canada we would close some Friday night fellowship meetings by singing the old spiritual 'Kum Ba Ya, my Lord'. We would hold hands and all felt a sense of warmth and belonging as we sang. But afterwards we went our self-indulgent ways, usually ending up at the local coffee shop enjoying ourselves. The contrast with the origins of that song could not be more stark. It was Australian evangelist John Smith who reminded me that Kum Ba Ya was born out of pain and hardship. I imagine a mother of six sitting in her shack behind her owners' mansion in the Southern States. The husband is still out in the fields and their oldest daughter, just 13 years of age, lies across her lap hysterical with grief and physical pain. She has just been gang-raped by the plantation owner's son and his friends. Her mother has done all she could to tend her daughter's physical injuries, but feels helpless to tend her child's emotional and spiritual wounds. As she caresses her daughter's forehead with one hand, she stretches her other hand to heaven and cries the prayer, 'Kum ba ya, my Lord' – literally come by here, my Lord.

In a modern context Martyn Joseph and Peter Brooke's song 'Please Sir' captures some of the emotion miners' children feel when their fathers have been made redundant. It is a vivid and moving portrayal of a young man's rage as he sees his dad's dignity stripped away. 'Please Sir' and 'Kum Ba Ya' both come from deep within broken hearts.

As I reflect on these scenes I realise how shallow my words were when I sang 'Kum Ba Ya' as a prayer in the early seventies. I wasn't really interested in what God had to offer, beyond the slight improvements he had already brought to my life. I had been raised in middle-class security and I didn't really want a revolution; a few minor character changes were sufficient for me. In contrast, the powerless and oppressed, those wrapped in pain and suffering, have a deep dissatisfaction with the way things are. They cry out in desperation for the Kingdom of God to come – and God always hears their cry. I have a growing conviction that only those who have experienced some kind of pain and suffering, powerlessness or oppression, can really appreciate the Kingdom of God. It is these people who want revolution. The Kingdom of God is not a sub-culture, but a counter-culture; the Kingdom of God, dramatically different from, yet totally identified with the real world in which we live.

Back in Canada I wrestled with these thoughts; I wanted my life and ministry to be different as a result. I began to hunger for genuine adventure; the adventure that sets people free as they are captivated by the love of God; the adventure that begins and ends with the Holy Spirit mapping out the route. I had some Bible training, a taste of missionary work and an appetite for more.

I was raring to go as I knew God was calling me to

preach. Throughout my year in Mexico I had been preparing a sermon to preach at my dad's church on my return. I had become convinced that this sermon would be the instrument for God sparking revival in the church! I had read and prepared and eventually accumulated eleven pages of notes. My message concerned the urgency of mission and winning the lost; it was rousing stuff.

When my dad did ask me to speak I leapt at the chance. It was a missionary Sunday service and there were about ten experienced missionaries on the platform that day. I had rehearsed the message to cows grazing in Mexico. As the cows responded to my eleven pages, I'd felt tingles running down my spine. I knew that if they had souls they'd have trotted to the front at the end to give their lives to Jesus!

A congregation of missionaries and Canadian Christians was different. I started to read my sermon and my mouth went dry within ten seconds. Within thirty seconds I knew that I wasn't feeling any of the anointing I'd felt preaching to the cows. Then I realised I had read several pages without looking up from my notes. I glanced up to make eye contact and ended up reading a paragraph twice. I got through about half of the eleven pages and decided it was doing nothing. I wound it up and my father took over the preaching instead.

It was a difficult, but important lesson. God does call us to act on his behalf, but he can plant a dream many years before he equips us to act on that call. I had been called to preach, but I wasn't ready and God hadn't opened up the way.

The way forward for me was to work with Tim Kikos touring some small Canadian churches showing slides from Mexico and talking about John Eils' work. We drove a large station wagon which was big enough to carry my double bass which we called 'Big Bertha'. Fortunately a car roomy enough to accommodate Big Bertha was also big enough for us to sleep in on our travels, cutting down on expenses.

We billed ourselves 'Two Revolutionaries from Latin America'. Our strategy wasn't particularly well thought through, and had a touch of arrogance. We wanted to challenge complacency in the church. We would address the self-indulgent worship and the lack of interest in all that was happening outside church walls. Tim and I took turns to preach and, as neither of us had preached much before, we spent the whole of each day preparing for each evening meeting. At the first mission in Williams' Lake we had sung our whole repertoire of songs by the third night so had to compose some of our own. Neither of us was a singer so the songs were awful, but God seemed to reward our efforts by opening up new opportunities.

During that tour I met a young man from England called Clive Calver. The arrival of this British evangelist and a Canadian band which had worked for British Youth for Christ in England meant our Friday night's meeting was cancelled. But I was attracted by the spirit and fire of the BYFC team and by Clive's 'angry young man' image. I was challenged by them, little knowing that years later I would share platforms in England with Clive and would become the national director of the organisation he introduced me to that night. Of course I was familiar with Youth for Christ in Canada, as my father had been director of Youth for Christ in Saskatchewan, but this was my first contact with British Youth for Christ.

The rest of our 'revolutionaries' tour went well. We didn't speak in large churches, but several older ministers gave us a platform and encouraged us in spite of our youth and naivety. From there I went on to preach at my first Bible camp. Preaching twice a day for seven days taxed my limited experience.

After the summer I enrolled for a year's course at a Vancouver community college to study Political Science. Weekdays at the college dovetailed with work on Saltspring Island where I was made pastor of the Ganges Evangelistic Tabernacle, the church Dad had planted years before. It was a year of discipline and study, but I made many good friends and cultivated a better understanding of some of the world issues with which Christians need to grapple.

When the course finished in May 1978 I visited Europe with a friend called Gilbert McQuarry. We flew to London then made our way to Portugal to meet up with one of my father's friends, Hosea Pessoa, who was a senior leader in the Assemblies of God in Portugal. He travelled with us and we spent two weeks touring Assemblies of God with Hosea interpreting for us. Again, here was a gracious, older man who was willing to affirm the ministry of a novice.

After our Portuguese tour we set off round Europe as tourists with Eurorail passes, ending up back in England where my only contact was Dr Tony Stone, an evangelist who was, for many years, associated with the Billy Graham Association. I first met him in 1969 when my father conducted a mission at the church in South Wales where he was pastor. I had written to him before leaving home to say something like: 'You know my dad. I feel called to England. Could you set up a preaching tour for me?' I was cheeky as well as naive! He wrote back saying yes, but, in fact, he set up only a few meetings for me. His view was that, if God had called me to Britain, God would open up opportunities. He introduced me to key places and people like the Hockley Fellowship in Birmingham and Dave Kitchen in Lincoln. In the end I spoke almost every night at some place or another for about two months.

Visiting the Hollybush Fellowship, and meeting Jim and Cynthia Wilkinson who had bought Hollybush Farm, was particularly significant. It is a real oasis of refreshment. When I first went, the house meetings started by Jim and Cynthia had grown so that about a hundred people packed into an old granary building for praise and worship meetings. All kinds of supernatural things happened as people prophesied and were ministered to. It made a real impact on me because it was something fresh and unorganised, with no strategy behind it. God was moving supernaturally in the Yorkshire Dales, and his work continues there to this day. The story of Hollybush has been recorded in a book called *Miracle Valley*.

I returned from the European trip convinced that God had called me to Britain, glad that he had given me opportunities to minister and grateful for the support of the new friends I had made. New horizons were opening up in more areas of life than even I could have planned.

One of my first tasks back in Canada was to speak at a missionary service. After the meeting I came down from the platform and was walking up the centre aisle when a pretty young woman threw her arms round me as if I was a long lost brother. I was wearing my smart blue suit, the missionary's 'uniform'; Kande, having stopped in Hawaii on her way home from Japan, was well tanned and wore clothes that made the most of the tan. She was, in fact, Kande Bettschen who had just returned from Japan where her parents had served as missionaries for the previous twenty-five years. When I had last seen her she was twelve years old; now she was seventeen. The warmth of her greeting bowled me over, but it was some time before I began to see her with anything more than brotherly affection. In the meantime we became good friends.

On one outing with Kande, her older sister and my brother, as I drove out of a restaurant car park, the engine almost leapt out of the car's bonnet. The engine mounts had broken and the car was suddenly out of action. I had planned to set off that evening in the car on a week's holiday waterskiing with friends, but now had to stay at home. I spent the evening at the youth group prayer meeting. It turned out to be a real milestone in my Christian life.

God was doing some powerful things in our youth group at that time. We had been a group of about forty with activities largely focused on social events. But God had prompted us to spend time praying and the weekly prayer meetings were attracting over a hundred young people. They weren't structured events; they just went on for hours with God speaking to people left, right and centre. That night God homed in on our ambitions. The question he seemed to be asking all of us was: 'Are you willing to give up even the good things I've given you to be a true disciple and to do what I want you to do?'

One friend, Rob Lungren was about to get married. He had grown up in Africa and was planning to return there with Eleanor, his new bride. He turned to me with tears in his eyes and told me God was telling him that he had to be willing to give up even those plans to marry and minister in Africa. He was shivering, not with cold nor fear, but with awareness of the presence of God. It was as if God was probing all of us to discover our motives. For me the question was simple: 'Are you willing to give up preaching?' That was tough. I wanted to preach; I felt God had called me to preach; I had been well received in Canada; doors had opened up in Europe; I had an autumn preaching schedule lined up; people were beginning to recognise me as a young evangelist. I went to bed that night leaving the question unanswered. It seemed as if God was mapping out my future and no other paths seemed to be opening up. I was convinced I must be on course.

I was still in bed the next morning when the phone rang. My friend Lois worked for an aid organisation called Hope International (formerly Food for the Hungry). It was a Christian agency similar to Tear Fund in the UK and I was very impressed with their work. Phnom Penh, the Cambodian capital, had been captured by Vietnamese and rebel forces. Pol Pot, the Cambodian leader had been convicted in his absence of causing the death of three million people. The Boat People were flooding into Thailand and Hope International needed someone urgently to go and set up an emergency feeding programme with money from the Dutch government and milk from the Canadians. I was asked to call in at the office to discuss the need with the executive director Ron Allen. While I had been at the youth prayer meeting they had been discussing the growing crisis and, although the organisation wasn't used to acting impulsively or making appointments without getting to know recruits well in advance, Ron Allen said: 'God seems to have given us your name. Would you be willing to go?'

It hit me like a ton of bricks that God was giving me an opportunity to face the challenge of the previous night. I asked two questions: 'How soon?' and 'Will I be able to preach in Thailand?'

His answers were blunt. Departure was to be within two weeks and there would be no opportunities to preach. The venture was under the auspices of the United Nations High Commission for Refugees and no preaching or evangelism would be allowed. I knew that God never asks a question without giving us the opportunity to answer. I asked for time to pray about my response and to talk with my parents and church leaders about the opportunity. As I talked the job through, everyone seemed to think it was right to go. I phoned the next morning to tell Ron Allen I'd go.

I thought I was being given the opportunity to prove I was willing to give up preaching; I didn't think God would actually send me out to Thailand. But two weeks later I was on a plane to Bangkok.

9

The killing fields

In Thailand I learned things about myself, the church and God's world that have continued to shape me. Though Thailand was a frightening, wilderness experience, my life was enriched as a result and I'm glad that I had the privilege of working there.

The Vietnam war had ended officially with a cease-fire agreement in January 1973, but the withdrawal of American troops had left the conflict between North and South Vietnam unresolved. The Communist North Vietnamese finally triumphed in 1975 and an estimated 230,000 refugees left South Vietnam, many arriving in the Thai refugee camps.

Cambodia was also in a state of turmoil as the population had been forced into the countryside to reconstruct the economy. Reports were reaching the West of massive killings verging on genocide. Vast numbers of Cambodians were dying of hunger; hundreds of thousands of those who could escape were pouring over the border adding to the over-crowding in the refugee camps.

Refugees from Laos were also on the move. The CIA-funded war in Laos was over but the newly-created People's Democratic Republic seemed to have become totally dependent on Vietnam. Laotian people were on the run;

local fighting and border clashes were continuing throughout the region.

Thailand had also been affected by the years of fighting. Morality was particularly affected as American servicemen had used the country as a base throughout the conflict. Entire naval fleets had anchored off Pataya Beach outside Bangkok and tens of thousands of servicemen from the States had 'invaded' Thailand during time off. As a result the population of Thai prostitutes grew enormously and to this day Thailand is still one of the prostitute centres of the world.

My impressions of Thailand were gained, principally, from the border regions where most of the refugee camps were situated. Within a few months of my arrival in August 1978, the United Nations High Commission for Refugees had invited non-governmental organisations like Hope International to be involved in bringing aid and development into the refugee camps. I believe there were about a quarter of a million refugees in Thailand at the time. The Thai government was deeply concerned about their future and did not want the refugees to become permanent residents. Anyone who made it into Thailand was immediately detained in a camp. There were accounts of boat-loads of refugees reaching Malaysia and being pushed back out to sea by the authorities, so Thailand's refugee-camp welcome was humane in comparison.

I arrived in my tweed jacket, ill-prepared to face the sweltering heat and humidity, let alone the growing refugee situation. The problems seemed insurmountable as numbers of refugees were growing daily, without the corresponding flow of refugees to other countries. I was met by Robin, son of Dulal Borpujari, director of Food for the Hungry in Thailand. Food for the Hungry was the American agency through which Hope International then worked. He took me to the Asia Hotel about half a mile from the organisation's offices and explained that I'd be having a meal with Dulal and some of the other staff that evening. Having taken me to my room, he left me to rest.

The room was dark, illuminated by a flickering neon light from outside. The traffic noise from the street below was awful. As the air-conditioning wasn't working, I opened the window, but that meant the noise became almost unbearable. I lay in my darkened room with the fan twirling on the ceiling and began to sink into depression sparked by fear of the unknown. I had never been in a situation like this before. I'd never been anywhere Oriental. My family had contacts everywhere else I'd visited; now I didn't even have close Christian fellowship. I didn't realise the extent of the difference until later, but I felt I'd entered a long dark tunnel without even a pin-prick of light showing at the other end. I tried to call my parents, which was difficult. When finally I did get through I simply asked them to pray. With hindsight I realise that I had not had adequate time to prepare and anticipate change. The culture shock was overwhelming.

When I went down for the meal, Dulal was friendly and welcoming. I discovered that I was one of a team setting up supplementary feeding programmes. We would be working in different camps; Robin was assigned the largest camp Nong Kai with over 40,000 Vietnamese; three Bengali workers were assigned Laotian camps in the north and I was assigned a camp in the north west for Meo refugees from Laos. We were told that we would be travelling to our respective camps the following day for a reconnoitring trip and to establish contact with the other agencies. I sat hearing all the instructions numb and dazed. I wasn't even given an opportunity to rest and recuperate from the journey or to orientate myself; I was immediately plunged into the work.

On a positive note, I immediately hit it off with a lawyer and former freedom fighter from Bangladesh called Ferose. His father was a leading magistrate in Bangladesh. He was a Muslim and had fought in the civil war between East and West Pakistan before Bangladesh came into being. Ferose and I were much the same age and we agreed that he should accompany me to my camp to help me establish contacts. Then I would go with him to his. That way we'd widen our experience and support each other.

We caught a coach to my camp first, travelling for thirteen hours through the night to the Nan province. We then headed for the Governor's mansion with a letter of introduction from Dulal. He was well known as the chairman of the Non-Government Organisation committee which brought together representatives of forty different organisations to coordinate the activities with the refugees. As soon as I presented the letter we were supplied with a driver and a military escort to take us to the camp, about eighty kilometres away in the mountains. I discovered later that it was a guerilla war zone and the worst thing I could have done was to ride in a government vehicle with a military escort as they were the prime targets for guerilla action. But we were unaware of the danger as we travelled into the mountains. The scenery was lush and green with elephants lumbering down the roads to work in the fields. Although the region had been affected by war, it was stunningly beautiful.

We arrived at the Meo camp and I was introduced to members of the Tom Dooley hospital; Tom was a young American who was part of the Peace Corps, an organisation formed to mobilise young people to help in the Third World. His heart had been captured by the Laotian people, so he had built hospitals throughout Laos. When he died, a foundation was started to continue his work. I discovered that the Tom Dooley Foundation was already running a feeding programme, but they were happy to pass it over to us along with all the staff they used. The camp commandant was very helpful. He explained that there were 13,000 Meo people in the camp; colourful and proud people who had been ferocious fighters in Laos. They had been secretly funded by the CIA: so when the Communists had taken over they had become a target for genocide. Heartbreaking horror stories had emerged from Laos about the torture and persecution of Meo people. In spite of what they had been through, their sense of dignity and hope for the future was challenging.

To start my work I set up a bank account with the money I had carried with me and began looking for accommodation. We then returned to Bangkok before travelling to Ferose's camp. As the camp was on the Mekong River, which divided Thailand and Laos before flowing on through Cambodia, there were dozens of people swimming across, almost every day. Ferose's camp was larger than the Meo camp and was home mainly to non-tribal Laotians, farmers from the plains and workers from Vientiane, the Laotian capital which we could see just across the river.

Apart from the pressures of acclimatizing and implementing the feeding programme I was going through emotion turmoil unconnected with the daily challenges of the job. I had made a dreadful decision which nearly ruined someone else's life. Having committed myself to stay in Thailand for six months, I was terrified of the prospect. In my disorientated state, rather than drawing closer to God, I opted for a human solution and decided that the only way to survive was to get married. I reached back into the Canadian culture that I knew and identified a friend called Sue I'd dated once or twice in Vancouver. We got on well and I thought: 'If only I could marry her, I'd survive my time in Thailand.'

I consulted Dulal and asked him if he'd mind if I got married. Dulal asked all about Sue, who was a nurse, before agreeing it would be a good step. So I phoned her and asked her to marry me. It seems silly now, but I was desperate. We hadn't talked marriage at all. We hadn't even had a serious relationship, so my proposal came as a bolt from the blue. Fortunately she said no after praying about it for a few days; although it was a qualified no; she would come and visit me at Christmas and would consider my proposal then.

I'm really grateful for the wisdom and restraint that she exercised. I feel a deep sense of embarrassment whenever

I think of what I did. I soon felt trapped by that phone call and within a few weeks I began to regret it; not because of Sue but because I was becoming more secure and adapting to the way of life. I felt less need of a companion and no need to get married, but I knew I would have to face the consequences of my actions sooner or later. I put it to the back of my mind and got on with the job.

I did settle down and began to enjoy myself. I wasn't getting much Christian fellowship but in the village of Pua in Nan province where I made my base there were two missionaries and I became firm friends with one of them, called Dorothy. She was working with the Overseas Missionary Fellowship and had lived among the Meo people in Laos for many years radiating the love of God. She had fled Laos with the people and continued to work with them in the camps where she was revered by all who knew her.

Reflecting on Dorothy's life, I realise that only those who have experienced pain, suffering or displacement – being on the outside and persecuted – only they can really glimpse God's kingdom. There was something about the kingdom that Dorothy carried into every situation she faced. She knew her God and her life flowed from deep reservoirs of peace, security, joy, commitment and loyalty. Spending time with her was the only fellowship I had.

The group I lived with in my first few weeks in Thailand couldn't have been a sharper contrast to Dorothy. They were doctors from the Tom Dooley Hospital and living with them was like being on the set of the *Mash* TV series. They were all lovely people; full of wit; but their lifestyles contrasted sharply with Dorothy's godliness. Eventually I found a house to live in on the edge of Pua. A maid came in every day to clean, cook and keep house and an interpreter called Promma was assigned to live with me. He was the former director of an evangelistic organisation, but had had to leave under circumstances which were never explained to me. He could have done the job without me, but in fact had a dishonest streak which came to light later.

To get around, I bought a 125cc four-stroke Honda motorbike which was large by Thai standards. It was my pride and joy and made the daily, twenty-six kilometre trip from Pua through the mountains to the refugee camp, a real pleasure. The area around the refugee camp was alive with guerilla activity and I was not allowed to live any nearer than Pua, the closest secure village. My daily route was quite dangerous; in fact I nicknamed one S-bend 'Ambush Corner' as so many military vehicles had come under sniper fire there as they slowed down to negotiate the tight corner.

When I was not working with the refugees I established links with the local school teachers and we built a feeding station out of bamboo at the school. To relax I bought a football and on Saturday afternoons played matches with the teachers. Life quickly settled into an enjoyable routine. I'd get up and go down to the Post Office to collect any mail; then after eating breakfast I'd head for the camp to oversee the feeding programme, liaise with staff and develop further contacts. When I returned home in the evening I'd eat a rice-based meal and spend the rest of the evening with the hospital staff or Dorothy.

I was eventually assigned two other camps; one for 3–4,000 Vietnamese in Korat near Bangkok and a Cambodian camp at Surin which had about 10,000 refugees. The Cambodian camp was stark in contrast with the Meo camp. Although the Meo people had been subject to great persecution, the Cambodian Khmer people had suffered even greater evil. The Khmer refugees continued to live under death threats even in the camps which were infiltrated by members of Pol Pot's Khmer Rouge; refugees were frequently conscripted to go back to fight in Cambodia, known temporarily as Kampuchea. The refugees sat still for hours with glazed looks; it was oppressive.

Food for the Hungry had set up a self-help project in the Surin camp involving pigs and poultry. I knew nothing about livestock but the work in all three camps taught me several lessons in management. At the Pua camp I felt that the twenty-six young men who were used to distribute the milk every day without remuneration were being exploited so, shortly after I arrived, I began paying them a wage. Within a month they went on strike for higher pay. When you move someone from being a volunteer to being a staff worker you change their motivation! Although there is still a love of their work, that is no longer their prime concern.

Another lesson was learnt on the pigs and poultry project; it was all about motivation and incentive. The refugee families were given three hundred three-day-old chicks to raise until they were thirty-five days old. We would then sell them on the open market and pay the families a flat fee, no matter how many live chickens they returned or how fat they were. As a result the quality of poultry reared was very poor. A profit motive was introduced whereby they benefited from producing healthy, fat chickens. In addition, twenty per cent of the profits was kept back as insurance in case a family lost all their chickens through disease. That way they were guaranteed at least a minimum payment. As a result the quality of chickens improved enormously and there was a buzz about the farm as refugees were able to earn more money. They were thrilled to bits. I learned on the job and enjoyed seeing increased motivation and morale among the refugees.

Travelling, particularly on the long coach journey between Bangkok and Pua, was one of the worst aspects of my work. I made the trip most weeks on the way to other camps and to liaise with other team members. Although the coaches were luxurious, they were designed for short Orientals not Canadians. I counted the minutes of each journey until a doctor suggested I take some Valium to help me cope with the trip. So I took him up on his suggestion and the Valium seemed wonderful; I'd be in a semi-comatose state for the entire journey, but within a few weeks I was taking up to eight Valium tablets for each trip. As their effect seemed to be reduced I moved on to Mogadon, a fairly heavy-duty tranquilliser which can be bought over the counter in Thailand. I was soon popping up to five of those a night. Then I began to use them every night rather than just when I travelled. In early December other staff members began to comment that I was changing and was no longer alert. I realised that I was becoming psychologically hooked on these tablets and was constantly in a semi-drugged state. I stopped immediately, but realised how easy it is to become dependent on drugs or alcohol.

War was a more obvious threat than drug addiction. Troops often searched the hills around where I stayed to flush out Communist terrorists. One particular night I was awakened by the crackle of sniper fire just a mile from my house as two young soldiers were ambushed after returning their girlfriends to the local village. I stood at the shuttered window as they brought the corpses and placed them almost under my house. I was numb, not knowing what to feel. It was bizarre and almost unreal; two teenagers had just been killed. I felt I was on the side of the soldiers, but I couldn't help feeling that there must be real roots of injustice to cause such anger among the guerilla fighters; they obviously believed that the system was wrong and were prepared to risk their lives to change it.

Communicating adequately with people back in Canada was difficult. The church in the West is so often insulated from the pain in the world. In my letters home I lobbied churches to sponsor immigrants from the refugee camps. Although I knew people at home were praying for me, I was aware of their indifference to the plight of the refugees. There is much in the world which breaks God's heart; he sees every child cry; every terrified father leading his children across the Mekong River; every pregnant mother who is bludgeoned to death. The church isn't hearing the cry, but God is. The authentic Gospel needs to be released from the four walls of our churches. I realised in Thailand that to pray while enjoying freedom from the pain of others is not following in Jesus' footsteps. Pietistic rituals do not satisfy God's demands, who summons us to care for widows and orphans. I began to feast on the Psalms and be challenged by the Gospels. The Psalms fuelled my appreciation of the greatness of God and the Gospels and his concern for his world.

Two experiences with Christians working in Thailand have had a lasting effect on my understanding of the church's role in relief work. The first encounter was with the Roman Catholic Archbishop of Ottawa, Archbishop Plourde. To lead the way in sponsoring Boat People coming to Canada he adopted a 15-year-old Cambodian boy. When the Archbishop came to Thailand to collect the boy I was assigned by the Canadian Embassy to assist the Embassy's immigration officer in welcoming the Archbishop. We had a wonderful time together although we nearly lost the boy before the Archbishop arrived as he had applied for refugee status to seven different countries under seven different names and was living under the name he'd assumed for the American embassy. We were worried he had been kidnapped and taken back to Cambodia by Pol Pot's forces. It was an embarrassment that the Archbishop was adopting a liar, but he was a very gracious and understanding man.

To mark the Archbishop's visit we threw a dinner for him and invited the Governor of the State and several other VIPs. I was a young man in my early twenties so this was all very heavy stuff for me; I was rather awe-struck by all that was happening and the people I was relating to. But the Archbishop arrived an hour early to chat with me as another man of the cloth. (By this time I was an ordained minister in a Pentecostal church in Canada.) He talked with me on my level and he shared with me about his spiritual pilgrimage, then asked me to tell my story. When I talked to him about my faith in Jesus and my struggle with church structures he recounted a story to me about the Flower Power days when he had picked up a hitch-hiker. This young man had asked the Archbishop 'Tell me why I should live. All you talk about is love and all I see is war. The church talks about peace and I see unhappiness everywhere. Tell me why I should live.'

The Archbishop told me he responded: 'Young man I have a doctorate degree in philosophy, but philosophy has given me no answers to life and no reason to live. I have attained high level within the Church, but the Church itself has given me no reason to live. My only reason for living is my personal relationship and faith in Jesus Christ who is my saviour.'

This was devastating to me, for although to this day there are many aspects of the Roman Catholic faith which I cannot understand, this man's personal faith and integrity challenged me deeply. I was profoundly moved by his love for God, and full of admiration for the fact he had not been compromised by the high political office he held within the most powerful ecclesiastical structure in the world. I sensed something authentic about this Archbishop and we have kept in contact occasionally since; every few years he sends me a snapshot of his Cambodian son.

Adopting just one boy from the thousands of desperate refugees in Thailand might seem like a drop in the ocean, but the Archbishop's gesture demonstrated his willingness to make a life-long commitment to bring about change. His action led the way for many other similar, apparently small steps which Canadian citizens took in opening their homes to refugees. Together those steps make an impact.

In contrast, the other church project I was exposed to in Thailand was an initiative of the right wing evangelical church of America. I see myself as an evangelical but could not align myself with what I witnessed.

A tele-evangelist ministry in America had offered to donate a large sum of money to Food for the Hungry to help with the work among refugees. Their way of raising money for refugees in Thailand was to send a choir to film a Christmas special from the refugee camps; they then used the graphic images of squalor and starving children to attract cash through their television programmes. Because I was the only evangelical working with Food for the

Hungry in Thailand at the time I was assigned the task of organising their tour.

The group wanted to distribute blankets and Bibles to 10,000 families and toys to 30,000 children along with Christmas meals for those children. We gave kites to the boys and dolls to the girls, but within a few hours the kites were in shreds and the dolls were limbless. Buying the Bibles was controversial as it seems we depleted the entire Thai supply of Laotian Bibles so other Christian agencies had to do without until fresh supplies could be printed. Yes, blankets and Bibles were put into the hands of needy people, but I'm not sure that the bulk of that initiative was very effective or worth doing.

The initiative was a waste of time and effort. The project made the group feel good, and made their audiences back home give as a response to what they saw. But it didn't change any lives in a lasting way. I felt grieved by the refusal of the tour party to address cultural issues. Everything was done for the television cameras. I'm not denying the good intentions and the motives of the young people when they came to sing, but it was heartbreaking to see thirty American Bible college students getting up to sing in their $300 suits, on stages stacked with expensive, high-tech equipment, singing Christmas carols in English to 10,000-strong crowds of refugees who couldn't understand what was being sung. The crowds simply came because they had never seen a spectacle like it.

When the Christmas meal was served in one camp, a riot nearly broke out. Children were crammed up to the door waiting to get their meal and their toy. I rescued one child who had fainted in the crowd and was being held up by the crush. The television cameras were whirring and one of the crew said, 'Isn't this wonderful, they are even fighting for the gifts we have for them.' He saw it as a great success, but I saw it as a gross obscenity. The cultural imperialism was deeply offensive. The Roman Catholic Archbishop was more challenging than these missionaries from America who gave out of their riches, but did not change in any way as a result. The incident made a lasting impression on me.

Sue came at Christmas. It was great to see her, but we quickly realised that we were two strong-willed people and were not compatible. It was painful to work through our relationship while she was there as we realised the mistake I had made. She stayed in Thailand when I left in February and was assigned to work as a nurse in my camp in the north. She did return to Canada in April and is now happily married to a Christian man, but we have never recovered the friendship that we had before I moved the goal posts.

I returned to Canada at the end of February 1979 with a wealth of experiences to think through. The Cambodian capital, Phnom Penh had just been captured by Vietnamese forces and Vietnamese Boat People were pouring into Hong Kong; little had been resolved politically and the prospects for the refugees had changed very little since I had arrived in Thailand, but I had been changed by the experience. It had been an enriching time, but also a dry wilderness. I had missed out on Christian fellowship and had had no consistent worship or teaching. I had learned positive lessons about management and drug dependency, but felt empty in many ways; embarrassed that I was leaving Sue and guilty for bringing her out there in the first place. I was enraged at the Western church for its refusal to take seriously the issue of displaced people in Thailand; I felt I had to do something about it but was uncertain what direction my life should take next or whether I would ever preach again.

10

Adventurer's rebuke

My rage at the indifference of the Western church may have been justified, but my own attitudes still needed drastic refinement. When I returned to Canada the Boat People were coming to the attention of the media so Hope International asked if I would work for them as their Western representative talking to churches and the media about the refugees' needs. My role was to tour the country speaking in churches, appearing on radio phone-ins, TV shows, and being interviewed for newspaper articles.

Staff changes at Hope International meant Ron Allen's role as Executive Director was passed to a Baptist minister called David McKenzie who has led the organisation ever since. David was responsible for one of the most painful moments in my life, but also a moment that shaped me. I had moved offices and had decorated my new one with some of the artifacts I'd collected in Thailand and Mexico. I settled myself proudly behind the desk with the 'Lowell Sheppard museum' all around me; then David arrived. He looked me in the eye, then looked around the office and said, 'Lowell, this office stinks.' He waited to see what my reaction would be, then said, 'This is not what it's all about,' and left me to stew.

I was angry and upset and thought I'd been

misunderstood. How dare he question me? But that night I cleaned everything out and I am grateful that he was courageously blunt with me. It made me rethink my life and my motivation towards ministry. Spending seven months in Thailand hadn't made me into any kind of hero or star. Identifying with needy people was nothing to do with pinning their art work to my wall like trophies. I needed to walk with humility, hungry for more of God and his rule. Things that other people would learn from Scripture, I had to learn from painful confrontation. Since then David has become a trusted friend and mentor. The word that he has stressed to me is 'integrity'. We are called to integrity in what we do and in our attitudes and motives. My 'museum' had put me in the same camp as the TV show fund-raisers. Before pointing to the 'speck of dust' in the eye of the Western church, I needed to deal with the 'plank' which distorted my own vision.

Travelling across Western Canada appearing on TV chat-shows and in churches, I felt right out of my depth. However, I felt I contributed what I could towards raising public awareness of the Boat People's plight. Although Canada never took on its full responsibility in welcoming the refugees, it made great strides to alleviate the suffering of some. Christians in Canada were linked with Boat People, particularly as the Canadian government agreed that churches could sponsor as many refugees as they felt able to care for if they assumed financial responsibility for the refugees' air fares and up to two years' welfare. Many Cambodian refugees came to Canada under this scheme and were given sanctuary, not just a house to live in, but spiritual and personal support. As one of many activists getting the issue into the press, I felt that this period of my life had been fruitful and productive.

In February 1980, while I was still working with Hope International, I went to Upper Volta, to visit my friends Rob and Clark Lungren and to see their land management project. Upper Volta, which has been known as Burkina Faso since a coup in 1983, is the third poorest country in the world. Clark and Rob were missionaries who were working with the people to halt the desertification of the country. There were desert regions in the north which were impenetrable forests only fifteen years ago. Their work has received international acclaim.

One aspect of the project aimed to fight the famine in the Sahele region of West Africa by raising antelope and deer; several different species could be grazed on the same pasture because they each eat different species of grass. With that nugget of an idea they were able to gain launch capital from the Canadian International Development Agency (CIDA) and from Hope International. We visited the project on behalf of Hope International five years after they had started. My brother Brent came along as the trip's photographer and we were joined by a vet, Terry Huberts, who has since served as Secretary of State for Economic Development in the Canadian provincial government of British Columbia.

We had a wonderful time over the three weeks we were there. We landed in the capital, Ouagadougou, then drove for eight hours into the bush. This involved travelling for four hours on a rough road and a further four hours ploughing through the bush to where Clark and Rob's camp was situated. They had been given a thousand square kilometres of land and their task was to rehabilitate the ecosystem in that area. We were struck by the commitment of the two families: Rob, Clark and their wives. They lived in the bush in windowless huts with no running water. They had neither televisions nor radios. Their communication with the outside world was infrequent. The eight-hour journey to town meant shopping trips were restricted to once every two months.

However, their costly, sacrificial lifestyle was paying off and, by the late eighties their venture was being described as the most successful ecological project of its kind in this half of the century. Its success has been seen in the return of elephant and giraffe to the region after fifty years. Clark and Rob are now using the same model to conduct feasibility studies for five new game ranches in West Africa, sponsored by the World Bank.

As well as checking on the progress of the project we worked with them building a dam and travelling through the region. On one anti-poaching patrol, we found an elephant shot by poachers. Rather than leave the carcass to rot it was butchered for the local people; my vet friend is unique among Canadian vets as the only one to have done an autopsy on an elephant! We returned home inspired by the way two visionaries had invested their skills in bringing life where death had begun to gain ground. Their practical witness, alongside their testimony, was a life-changing mix which embodied the fullness of God's good news.

In contrast to the reconstruction and rejuvenation we saw in Upper Volta, the church situation we returned to in Canada was divisive and potentially destructive. My father had been going through a very difficult period at the Evangelistic Tabernacle in Vancouver after seven years as the senior pastor. For two years there had been a small element in the church who felt that his time was up. This group wanted a Bible teacher rather than an evangelist. Some had expressed concern that dad was turning the church into a mission. Lots of people were being converted from the streets which, from many of the young people's point of view, was fantastic but a few of the more established members were not so sure. A vote of confidence showed dad had seven per cent less than the sixty-five per cent required support.

We got back home in time for his last Sunday service. His final sermon focused on the need to win the lost and he focused on the positive outcome of the vote, interpreting it as an indication that he should return to work as a full time evangelist. But several members of the fellowship wouldn't hear of it. They wanted dad to continue as their pastor, so, after much agonizing, a new fellowship was formed, called the Bible Life Assembly. I continued working part-time with Hope International, but joined Dad as an associate pastor of the new church, with special responsibilities for church growth and evangelism.

We targeted people in the west end of Vancouver, conducting missions, meetings and street work. Our ministry focused on the most densely populated area of the city. Homes in the high-rise blocks were expensive, but on the streets, the people we met were prostitutes and homosexuals who had been rejected by the rest of society. Over the summer we had a meeting every Sunday night and saw, on average, three adults converted to Christ each week. We attracted people to the service with a mass mailing to all the apartments headlined 'Who cares?' Inside was a simple outline of the Gospel. We also sang and preached on the streets each Sunday before the services, then waited for the people to arrive. Although the responses were only in twos and threes, many were lasting conversions. Those who came to Christ in this way formed a housegroup in the area. My only regret is that we didn't plant a church in the district.

The other main outreach venture was the Honey 'n the Rock Cafe, a Gospel rock cafe in the upper dining-room of a restaurant called Honey's. This was situated in the Gastown area of Vancouver; the night club area of town. The programme, from 8pm to midnight each Friday, included a variety of Gospel bands playing jazz, rhythm and blues and light rock. Once a month we held a variety show with local churches supplying the talent which brought in Christians from a wide range of churches, but nearly half of those who came along had no church connections. God seemed to be taking the walls off the church and many were becoming Christians as a result. It was here that I first met Johnny Markin, a young guitarist and songwriter, who has become a close friend and colleague.

However, I still felt schizophrenic as a Christian worker. Some of the time I was an evangelist, presenting Christ to people who didn't know him; at other times I was lobbying the church to care for the poor. I had not been able to integrate the two aspects of the Gospel in my life.

Work with Hope International continued to give me glimpses of projects to help the world's poor. One trip with my boss David McKenzie took me back to Africa, this time to Kenya and Zaire. In Kenya we flew up the Rift Valley to the Turkana region to visit a Canadian missionary couple called the Herrods at a feeding station in the famine belt. Normally proud, nomadic people, the Turkana had been affected by the famine which had blighted vast areas of East Africa. The landscape which confronted us on our arrival was like a lunar scene, it was so bare and windswept.

Wayne Herrod met us and escorted us to a large compound surrounded by thorny shrub. Five thousand Turkana people had been herded into the compound and, as each one left by the narrow exit, they were given their meagre daily ration. The barbed wire ensured that no one was fed twice, but I was horrified to see people being treated like cattle. One woman came up to us and held out the baby in her arms. It was impossible to gauge the child's age as it was so malnourished. Its head fitted into the palm of its mother's hand, its arms and legs dangling down on either side like dead leaves. As I had a camera the woman assumed I would take a photograph and they might be given more to eat as a form of payment. The incident convinced me that taking pictures of starving children is immoral; it robs them of all dignity and only serves to manipulate Western emotions into making a superficial, one-off response.

It was hell to be there. God didn't seem near. As we walked back to the dusty airstrip, I looked at Wayne, his mouth scarred by heat sores, skin hanging on his bones. He had brought his wife and family to what seemed to me to be a God-forsaken place. 'Why don't you leave? It's a hopeless situation,' I asked. We both knew that giving people food was not a long-term solution, but what else could be done? His reply was stark and simple: 'This is where God has placed me and, if I'm anywhere else I know that I'll be neither happy nor fulfilled.' Certainly his family looked happy, but I was glad to be leaving.

The dust and despair seemed doubly cruel the next day as we flew to north east Zaire. The flight took us over thousands of acres of land owned by a multi-national food company producing pineapples. Evidently the world is capable of feeding the hungry. We in the West cannot avoid all blame by pointing to wars and mismanagement; we will have to answer for what our greed has done.

In Zaire, the first centre we called on was home to a large group of missionaries. The most memorable aspect of the visit was the pilot's comment as we flew in: 'Missionaries are like manure,' he said. 'If you spread them around they do a great job, but if you pile them up in one place it begins to smell a bit!' It didn't take an expert to see that he was right. Politics and personality clashes between individuals and the organisations they represented diluted the value of working together and pooling resources.

We also visited Imeloko in the heart of Zaire which had been founded by the European medical missionary Paul Carlson who had been martyred during the revolution in the Congo. The hospital he had founded was highly acclaimed for its work with leprosy sufferers. Although we were shown round the medical compound our task in Imeloko was to monitor a fish farming project which was proving to be highly successful.

The fish chosen for the project reproduced rapidly and provided vital protein for villagers. Families simply built a fish pond and we stocked it with a supply of fish together with guidelines on their care. Initially thirty ponds were funded by Hope International, but they were so successful that other villagers didn't wait for us to get involved; they dug their own ponds and stocked them with surplus fish from their neighbours' ponds. They weren't using the correct procedures or technology, but there were more than five hundred fish ponds in the area when we visited; the initiative had proved to be an unqualified success.

We were entertained by the villagers who, unnecessarily,

carried a table into the bush so we could eat beside one of the fish ponds. A meal of fish would have been wonderful, but they offered us huge platefuls of putrid, sludgy stew, which I assume was a local delicacy. David and I were the only ones eating; our hosts just looked on. I managed to get every mouthful down so as not to offend, but to my horror, they then brought another plateful. I later discovered that if you clean your plate, they assume you are still hungry! I couldn't finish the second helping, but fortunately that signified that I was satisfied. It was an unforgettable experience.

Finally, work with Hope International took me to a third continent and provided an opportunity to gain much more hands-on experience, this time building a centre for nutritional education on a dung heap next to a Peruvian shanty town. A team of volunteers were recruited from my own church and through Hope International. The mix of backgrounds, maturity and belief – some were not Christians – stretched my management skills to the full and taught me several new lessons.

The centre was to serve about 2,000 shanty-town families who lived on the outskirts of Lima. Our building site was basically the toilet area for the whole community. Although tourist books say it hasn't rained in Lima for 100 years, there is a sprinkling of rain from time to time, but the area we were working in did look like a moonscape. To lay the foundations for the building we had to dig through a thick layer of dust and dried human excrement; to say it was a filthy job is an understatement! Some Mormons living across the alley from us left each morning with their smart blue suits, smelling of soap and after-shave. In sharp contrast, we were unshaven and, despite great efforts, could not shift the smell that clung to us.

We worked alongside a Peruvian bricklayer and my job was to manage the team. There were stresses and strained relationships as different motives surfaced during the fortnight's work. Some of the team knew they were there to work and put in a solid eight-hour day; others wanted to see the sights of Peru; some worked virtually unsupervised, others needed lots of encouragement; some wanted to spend time together in prayer and Bible study; others were less keen.

In spite of the difficulties we finished the clinic in record time and spent the rest of our month on another project building bee-hives in the Amazon jungle on the other side of the Andes. There were several administrative hiccups which proved frustrating, particularly the shortage of work for us to do. After the intensity of the project in Lima, job satisfaction was low. However, the experience of jungle life was enriching and enabled us to see first-hand how economics can affect a community. The people had been prosperous pepper farmers, but international price fluctuations and Peru's seventy per cent inflation rate had forced the farmers deep into debt. As bank interest rates were running at a massive sixty per cent they felt helpless in the face of economic forces beyond their control. With hindsight it is easy to see how Latin American farmers, faced with even worse situations today, decide to grow drug crops which fetch high prices on the world market.

My work with Hope strengthened my conviction that if we claim to be citizens of God's Kingdom, we will care for and reflect his bias to the poor. We must be concerned with justice, mercy and have compassion for individuals helping them find forgiveness and acceptance by God. Although I was involved in work caring for the poor, I felt as if I was only flirting with the needy; I could fly back to comfortable Canada whenever I wanted. The people I met in Thailand, Africa and Peru did not have that luxury; they are trapped by their poverty. The challenge to identify with the poor, as Jesus identifies with us, remains a lasting lesson from my work with Hope; a lesson which I am still working through.

11

Love, sex and marriage

While work with Bible Life Assembly and Hope continued, I was setting off on another life-long adventure. Relationships with girls had never gone smoothly for me. My teenage infatuation with Cindy had left me hurt and defensive and the near-catastrophe with Sue in Thailand left me wishing that arranged marriages were a Western as well as Eastern tradition!

When I returned from Thailand I knew that marriage to Sue would not work out. However, friends back home were still convinced that she would make a wonderful pastor's wife. I felt guilty for encouraging her to go to Thailand and continued to feel responsible for her until she returned home, but we had both realised our relationship had no future. Back in the secure environment of home I felt no particular need for a wife and was happy to remain good friends with the girls I knew.

Unknown to me, on the night Kande Bettschen threw her arms round me in a welcome-home hug after the church service, she went home and asked her sister Lorna to pray with her that she would marry me. Our two families were very close so Kande and I saw a lot of each other and became firm friends. I even chatted with her parents about my arranged marriage theories: in Thailand I had seen the strength of marriages where commitment is emphasised more than love, and the commitment is seen as two families join forces.

I'd made a mess of relationships up to that point. I'd found it difficult to stay casual and friendly; I'd become too serious too quickly. But now I had decided to end that chapter of my life. I was not going to get involved romantically, but rather enjoy life and make sure that integrity was the watchword in all relationships. So, even though I began to see Kande almost every other day, we were like brother and sister, having lots of fun but not getting serious.

After a while Kande began to pray that our friendship would take a more serious turn; if it didn't she had decided to spend less time with me. Only a few days later I turned down her invitation to go out for coffee and, instead, went to spend the evening with a bunch of single guys who had just moved house. Kande went home convinced that there was no future for our friendship. I discovered when I got to my friends' house that I wanted to be with Kande. So I phoned her and asked a corny question: 'Would you like to go to the park to watch the submarine races?' She never asked what we'd do 'til the submarines surfaced! I'd once overheard her telling a friend that she would never let a lad kiss her unless he asked her permission first. When it came to the moment to ask her, my knees were knocking; it's one thing to practise in front of a mirror at home; the real thing's a lot more unnerving. But she said yes, I didn't miss, and the rest is history . . .

Asking Kande out was one thing; convincing her parents that she was the right girl for me seemed much harder. They liked me and saw me as a son, but they didn't feel Kande would make a good pastor's wife. However, I didn't want someone who could play the accordion, preach and pastor better than me. In persuading them that I wasn't looking for a conventional pastor's wife, I became even more convinced that Kande was right for me.

We got engaged in September 1980 more than a year

after that trip to the park. I had always felt that a short engagement was best and that we shouldn't get engaged until we were ready for marriage, so as soon as the engagement was announced we arranged the wedding for 27 December that year.

When I finally made the commitment to Kande, I came to the conclusion that it had to be a commitment to being vulnerable, to sharing and to feeling what the other person feels. When I am concerned about myself, only those things which directly affect me are of any importance. But when I fell in love with Kande I found that I had a new set of problems. Suddenly I found that things which wouldn't have concerned me at all were causing me pain because they caused her pain. When we had children it was the same – I feel deeply the pain of my children.

Relationships are important because God doesn't want us to go it alone. God himself is committed to a relationship in the Trinity. The creation of Adam and Eve also illustrates God's commitment to relationships. The emphasis on cities throughout Scripture – as we move from a garden to a city – shows God's commitment to community and relationship. And yet, as well as being committed to relationships, God enjoys the distinctives that we each have.

Understanding God's perspective on relationships helps us appreciate the Bible's teaching on sex. Often the strictness of Scripture on this subject is seen as an attempt to suppress natural inclinations, labelling them as sinful. But it is quite the opposite. The strictness of Scripture on the subject of sex is not to suppress, but rather to safeguard the dignity of the individual.

One church I have preached at objected to the way I talked abut sex. I used the word 'screw' to describe the sex act between people who are only interested in selfish pleasure. I used the word deliberately and qualified what I said by explaining that I refused to say they were 'making love' as that would only grace their vulgar act with a sense of purpose. All their two bodies were doing was grinding against each other for personal pleasure. Therefore the word that is used on the streets to describe the act has, I think, much more integrity.

Making love is all about commitment, obligation and sticking by one another. A key problem in relationships, one which I struggled with as a teenager, is that we want to go a mile towards intimacy but only an inch towards commitment. Often courting couples ask 'How far can we go?' Scripture is very clear that the act of intercourse is only allowed within a permanent, committed relationship. But, of course, there are levels of sexual activity, from writing poems and making eye contact to heavy petting. Every Christian young person struggles with the question of 'How far can I go?' I agree there are grey areas, but I believe our level of intimacy must always match our level of commitment. It is helpful to think in terms of three road signs: the one furthest away says 'Authorised Personnel Only'; Scripture is clear that intercourse can only take place between people who are authorised to have intercourse, and they are a man and a woman who are married to each other. There is a second sign, closer than the first, which says 'Do Not Enter'. An individual has no right to enter into a private area of another individual's life, either emotionally or physically, without first making a permanent commitment to stand by their side and support them through thick and thin. Finally, the nearest sign says, 'No U-Turns' for we all know the point in our sexual relationships as single people where we reach a point of no return. That may be holding hands or a passionate kiss, but there's no turning back and we quickly slide past the other two signs violating Scripture and ourselves as well. Ultimately, however, the question 'How far can I go?' is the wrong one. Rather we should be asking 'How can I preserve and increase this individual's sense of dignity?' for dignity is God-given.

I have come to understand that there is a noble side of jealousy. Often we describe God as a jealous God, but that leaves us confused because we see jealousy as something connected with our fallen nature. But there is a jealousy which is noble and stems from having a monopoly or sole-ownership. If I find another evangelist preaches better than I do, I am not justified in being jealous because he or she has every right to be better than I am. But if another man begins to gain the affections of my wife, then I am justified in being jealous. Jealousy can be destructive, so what we do with it is important. When we make someone or something else our top priority God's jealousy is justified. He has rights of sole-ownership which we betray at our cost.

Kande and I have had difficulties in our marriage, not to the point of breaking up, but because of the clash of our two very strong wills. When we were first married I went off to Africa for four weeks and came back to find Kande had adapted to being a single woman again. Not that she was out dating other men, but because she had become accustomed to doing what she wanted, making her own decisions about what to do and how to spend her money. In every marriage there is turbulence, like when two rivers converge. The end result can be chaos or a mighty streaming force. After twelve years of marriage Kande and I are finding our relationship more beautiful, more productive and more exciting. We each have our own careers; she supports me and I her. Our marriage is becoming more sound and beautiful, though we still have to work at it. But I have discovered that even in a good marriage, the primary relationship is the vertical one – with God. It is only when that is sound that all the secondary, horizontal relationships become healthy as well.

Kande has proved to be perfect for me. She makes up what I lack and I get a real charge from seeing her grow and develop in areas independent of me. She now runs a successful consultancy helping businessmen and women relate effectively to their Japanese counterparts. I love her and am immensely proud of her.

12

Turned on to evangelism

Our first home was a rented flat in a high-rise apartment block. Kande continued working for a Japanese doctor and I carried on my work with Bible Life Assembly and Hope International. My four-week trip to Africa with David McKenzie came shortly after we were married, which was not an ideal time as we were still adapting to married life. When I returned home Kande had readjusted to making her own decisions rather than sharing life with me, so we had to work at being a couple again, but good marriages are worth working at.

The trip to Peru involved a similar separation. Kande had considered coming along, and I was disappointed when she decided to stay in Canada as I wanted her to share the experience. But, in some ways it was better as the responsibility of leading a team of twelve put me under a lot of pressure.

I came back from Peru tired and exhausted. For the next year, I concentrated on work with Bible Life Assembly and the Honey 'n the Rock Cafe. But I knew that my time with them was coming to an end. Kande felt positive about leaving, but I was the one who felt we were being called to England. We did pursue a number of options as we wanted to be open to God: we had been asked to consider pastoring a church in Canada; secondly we knew we could work in the Third World with Hope International or another mission agency, or, thirdly we could come to England.

The first two options were being suggested to us and actually seemed more concrete alternatives as we had no invitation to Britain, but felt convinced that God was calling us. If that was the case I knew Kande would have to agree. In May 1982, Kande and I brought a team of young people to the UK and toured for three weeks. Kande loved it and knew right away that this was where God wanted us to be. She saw some similarities with Japan, both being densely populated island nations, I suppose, and, surprisingly, she felt at home.

When we returned to Canada the church agreed to give us a tenth of the financial support we would need. They also encouraged us to commit ourselves to a year in Britain in case it didn't work out. We agreed, though we knew we were coming to Britain permanently. We finished work with Bible Life Assembly in September 1982 and spent the autumn travelling in an effort to raise further support as well as seeing our families. In January 1983 my parents drove us to Seattle and we set off for London.

We were met by Bob Reynolds. On my first trip to Britain in the 1970s Bob and his wife Jackie had become like a brother and sister; they have now become firm friends. Our first stop was Stourbridge where we now live. We came with the promise of some financial support from our church, but no other income. All we had in the diary was a four week tour of Portugal in March and a week's holiday at Spring Harvest in April as guests – Bob had said 'Come to Spring Harvest and see what God is doing in Britain.' Also Tony Stone handed me three mission invitations he'd had; one in Aberystwyth, Wales; one in Dundee, Scotland and a third in Port Glasgow organised by Bill Hogg, a Scottish young man. We also had a three week tour with a Canadian rock band called Jubilation during May and June.

The Port Glasgow mission was town-wide and received coverage in the *Christian Herald*, on Radio Clyde and in the *Glasgow Herald*, which was awesome for me at the time. I tried to put into practice some of the lessons I'd been learning by combining social action with evangelism, putting a real emphasis on the unemployment problem. The issue we tackled was 'Jesus in the Dole Queue'. I spent time with the local Industrial Chaplain; spoke in factory cafeterias and in the shipyards and worked with young people on the council housing estates. It was the most remarkable mission I'd ever been involved in. By the final night crowds had grown to 800 which was incredible for an unknown Canadian evangelist at a mission organised by a local youngster. On the final night when we sang 'Our God Reigns' we almost took the roof off, there was such a sense of God's blessing and power. God alone knows the lasting impact of the mission, but the most strategic aspect of the mission for me was my friendship with Bill Hogg who is now a Youth for Christ evangelist in Scotland.

Apart from fulfilling the few commitments we had, we spent time getting to know different people and their ministries. We followed the principle I'd learned many years before: 'Never worry about your ministry because a ministry will always make room for itself.' So we didn't go lobbying, but God began to open doors. When September came I was praying about the following year and had one of those rare moments when God gave a vision and a plan. He seemed to say very clearly: 'Next autumn put together a youth team and prepare to do missions.' The team was to have street workers and schools workers, like a commando team to raid enemy territory. God also seemed to say: 'Get yourself a yellow mini-bus and fit it out for the equipment.'

Twelve months later I had the team and the yellow mini bus. When God gave the plan he didn't tell me where we'd be working, but three weeks later Ian Green of the National Youth Council of the Assemblies of God asked if I would give them September to December 1984 to do fourteen, week-long youth missions. When Ian phoned me to ask me to put together the team, I could hardly believe it. I had heard from God!

So I put together a team of twelve people called Harvest United using Phil Collins, a trainee evangelist converted under Tony Stone. He headed the street team with Julian Stone, Tony's son; Tim Mitchell, a Canadian evangelist and Kande. They were dynamic on the streets. My brother Brent led the schools team with his wife Tracy and Mark Goodyear who had responded at an Assemblies of God conference when I appealed for dramatists. A young person came from Canada every three weeks to join the team and together we held missions throughout Britain from Cornwall to Scotland and Wales to the east of England. We were exhausted by the end of the three months and totally drained.

Kande's involvement came as a surprise to her. Initially she travelled with me, only to be a support. She did try to be my secretary for a time but has never enjoyed typing and very soon she got into colour analysis which has occupied her from time to time since then. Joining the street evangelists team with Harvest United helped her find a ministry of her own. The first girl she talked to she led to Christ and she quickly developed her own identity as a street evangelist. Kande was also concerned with setting up home. We thought we would live in the Midlands but on a visit to the Hollybush Fellowship we discovered that Jim Wilkinson had a vacant cottage on his farm, so it became our home for three years and Hollybush supported us in many ways as our base fellowship.

After the initial three-month tour, Harvest United continued. My brother and his wife left but Carl and Jane Gidney joined us. He was formerly an Elim minister and came to Hollybush as guests with Carl's parents. As soon as we met, I knew we would work together. They soon joined us and lived with Kande and me for a year working with Harvest United around the country.

The financial miracles which made Harvest United

possible stand out as milestones in that year. By the end of April 1985 the Fiat I had bought was using a pint of oil every 100 miles; its days were numbered. We had three months of mission coming up in Scotland so I prayed about it. It seemed as if I had just enough faith to believe that God would keep the car running for those three months. God answered and it didn't need any extra oil for the Scottish trip; the team named it Lazarus for obvious reasons.

But after the mission, Terry and Dale Huberts, friends from Canada offered to take us on a holiday to the French Riviera if Kande and I provided the wheels. I couldn't see them riding in a rust-ridden old Fiat all the way to the French Riviera so early in July, before they came, I began praying about the car. I felt it was about time to replace it and, as I had £1,000 saved and thought I could borrow about £3,000 from the bank, I began looking for a car under £4,000. A friend of mine, the treasurer of Harvest United, was an accountant with Austin Rover. His company car was coming up for sale as it had 15,000 miles on the clock and all company cars were replaced at that point. He negotiated the sale at £4,175 which was above my ceiling so I said I couldn't afford it. But he offered to lend us the car for the holiday and said 'Don't make your decision yet. Use the car and see it as a test drive.' So I took it on a 3,000 mile test drive through France!

When I came back I was convinced it was the car for me so I rang to say I would buy it. He then took it back to arrange the paperwork and several days later when it was ready for collection he explained that the company had re-appraised it and, because the mileage was higher, they had dropped the price to £3,875. I couldn't believe it, but God hadn't finished providing. An hour later a business man in Leeds rang to say my father had been visiting him and he had asked after me. When dad said I was in the process of buying a car, this business man felt God saying that he should buy the car for me. I thought he was simply offering to buy a £500 heap of junk so I nervously told him I had just agreed to buy a car at £3,875 and had £1,000 towards it. I thought he'd send me a gift of £500 to help pay for it. But that was not what he had in mind. He said: 'I don't care how much it is. God's told me to buy you the car of your choice. Are you sure you want the Montego?' I was amazed. I must confess a Porsche raced through my mind at that moment. A few days later we collected the Montego. The car was vital to get us from mission to mission. The whole incident taught me about faith and how faith has to be exercised to develop.

The second major financial miracle for Harvest United in August of that year helped develop our faith as a whole team. We had been invited to hold a Port Glasgow-style mission in Bulawayo, Zimbabwe, combining social action with preaching as part of a two-year programme of evangelism in the area. We needed about £5,000 to pay for the flights, so we agreed that each of us would raise our own fares and if any of us had a surplus it would go towards someone else's fare. If anyone didn't raise their fare we'd accept that as God's will and they'd stay behind in England.

Two weeks before we were due to pay for the tickets we still needed almost all of the £5,000. The night before, we still needed £1,200. Half an hour before, we still needed £800. But at 10am on deadline-morning I walked into the travel agent's office with all of the money. Every team member had seen their own miracle. We went to Zimbabwe and had a fantastic trip ministering with both blacks and whites. Zimbabwe was still adapting to the rapid changes brought about by the transfer of power from whites to blacks, so there was much need for forgiveness and reconciliation.

It was Kande's first experience of the Third World and she found it an enriching time. We preached in schools and at city-wide rallies, with a couple of thousand people attending the final rally in a park. Then we were treated to a three-day holiday at Victoria Falls; the Zimbabwean team had budgeted to pay us but we were not allowed to take currency out of the country so the holiday was their way of saying thank you.

Harvest United went back to Zimbabwe the following May for the culmination of the months of mission. By this time Kande was pregnant, expecting our first child, so she didn't come with us, but Tony Stone came, together with Peter Green of Christian Family Ministry, Mike Jones, another local evangelist, and my father. There were thirty of us in four different teams, conducting missions in churches all around Bulawayo, culminating in rallies at the Town Hall and White City Stadium. Many churches were renewed and money was raised for development in the rural areas.

After coming to Britain with no foreseeable income or ministry I was constantly encouraged by God's faithfulness to us. I'd been raised seeing God provide every penny for Mum and Dad, but I hadn't seen these kind of miracles for myself. Kande was also used to 'living by faith' when her parents were missionaries in Japan, but both of us had salaries in Canada. God does develop our faith to meet every challenge but, it seems as if each challenge is slightly greater than the previous one. Apart from the $200 a month we received from Bible Life Assembly which covered the costs of mailing lists, life insurance and pension arrangements in Canada, we were never reliant on money from outside the UK. As God provided all we needed to live on, we felt he was confirming our decision to come as immigrants rather than missionaries.

Moving abroad is like being born again in a psychological sense. Missionaries spend months or years preparing to go to another culture and, usually, they arrive and are picked up by another missionary, taken home and given a meal. They become bonded to that person and their missionary lifestyle rather than the local culture. It is far better to have a national pick you up at the airport and to spend at least six months becoming integrated in the national culture.

The cultural differences between Canada and Britain are not that great but I wanted to work on this principle of bonding, so spent as little time as possible with fellow North Americans so they became 'them' and British people became 'us'. We came as immigrants not as missionaries; we go back to Canada on 'holiday' not on 'furlough'. We made a determined effort to Anglicise; we have not fully crossed the bridge but I hope we do not seem to be foreigners. We are here to stay.

For the first few months it seems we were under spiritual attack and at times felt Satan accuse us of making a huge mistake: 'You don't have what it takes to reach British young people.' 'God won't pay your bills.' 'What if Tony Stone and others knew what you were really like.' But I became increasingly motivated to be an evangelist. I grew up with a stereotype of an evangelist as either a tele-evangelist asking for money or the evangelist who travelled around holding special meetings in churches which were attended mainly by Christians. My understanding of an evangelist was now being redefined.

Understanding the Biblical role of a herald-preacher, prompted my increased confidence and excitement in being an evangelist. The herald of Old Testament times was dispatched to proclaim new laws. It wasn't until the herald went into the market-place to make the proclamation that the law would have any effect; publishing the news was part of the legal process. An effective herald doesn't speak in legal jargon or a foreign language. The herald has to speak the language of the people so they hear clearly and understand what is required. It is in hearing and understanding that faith is unleashed, not merely in hearing. The church needs to communicate the message, so that the raw freshness of the Gospel cuts into people's lives.

I'm not the type of evangelist who feels compelled to preach every night; I feel called to administration and leadership as well. Yet when I have the opportunity to preach the Gospel to those who have not yet heard, I get a tremendous buzz and I have great confidence that God will use what I say. I don't feel the need to include all of the Gospel every time I preach; I may focus only on the Green issues which are at the forefront of many people's minds. Like Paul speaking to the people in Athens, I want to touch on topical and relevant issues. I am also concerned to preach with integrity, not leaping in and out of an area without offering people a tangible expression of on-going support and care. Finding creative ways to speak and to be Good News is a constant challenge.

13

Finding my place

Looking back on life's 'co-incidences' makes it possible to see how God has been working to prepare, discipline and provide. At the time there seems to be little to link the people we meet, the opportunities and the hardships we face, and the circumstances which seem to lead us one way or another. With the benefit of hindsight, seeing the way God has worked in the past encourages great confidence that he is continuing to map out our lives whatever we might face. Looking back I can see how so much of my learning experiences in Canada, Thailand, Africa and Peru played a part in preparing me for work in Britain. Harvest United was another major stepping stone, helping to equip me for the role which God opened up in British Youth for Christ.

My first encounter with BYFC had been meeting Clive Calver in Canada during the 1970s and, of course, my father had been a Youth for Christ evangelist in Saskatchewan so I was familiar with the international organisation. When Bob and Jackie Reynolds directed us to Spring Harvest in 1983, I saw BYFC in action again as one of the sponsoring bodies behind the event. It was a cold, wet Easter week, but I could see that Spring Harvest was playing a strategic part in what God was doing in

Britain. I popped into Tosh – The Other Spring Harvest – which was geared to young people and went to some of the celebrations and was quite impressed with what I saw, though I recognised that it's what you do when you get home that counts.

It was amazing to discover that the tall man with a large moustache leaping around the stage, dancing like I'd never seen anyone dance before, was the newly-appointed national director of BYFC. During one of the celebrations the team prayed over Rob, asking God to equip him for his new role. As they prayed I felt as if God dropped something very significant into my being. Like many ambitious young evangelists I could say 'I'd like to do that job', but sometimes you know when God has dropped something deep into your spirit. I felt God say to me: 'One day you will become national director of BYFC and one day you will be on the platform as one of the leaders of Spring Harvest.'

My spirit leapt with a sense of 'Yes that's right,' but I knew how ridiculous it sounded, so my mind was saying 'Down boy, that's ambition rearing its ugly head!' Rev Harder's words came back to me and I knew that if I was hearing God correctly, he would open the way. I shouldn't push doors. So I never did anything to get to know the BYFC team and was happy to be an evangelist working with Tony Stone.

I met Rob White at an evangelists' conference at the end of 1984. We felt a bond immediately and spent some time getting to know each other. Six months later, at an Assemblies of God conference in April 1985 after Harvest United was underway, we met again. This time he asked me some leading questions about joining BYFC. Basically I said yes, then he went on to explain that he was reorganising the leadership team and wanted a Director of Evangelism.

As BYFC is an evangelistic agency and evangelism is the focus of all the work it seemed strange to have someone singled out as a Director of Evangelism, but Rob said he wanted an evangelist with a strategic mind, pastoral gifts, and an ability to lead. I can't say I matched up to all of those specifications, but Rob said he had found what he was looking for in me. He asked me if I was willing to consider it. I was bowled over and flattered but also felt at peace as I identified closely with BYFC's aims and approach.

A few weeks later he phoned and invited me to apply for the job. Kande and I were interviewed by Steve Gaukroger, Pastor at Stopsley Baptist Church, who is also on the BYFC Board and by mid-August Rob rang to say the board was offering me the post. We met at a service station just south of Leeds on the M61 to go through the terms. He says he dreaded that meeting as he had not talked salary with me at all. It had crossed my mind, but I had assumed that there wouldn't be a salary and I hadn't raised the issue as I didn't want it to cloud Kande's and my thinking. He took me through the job description first, then told me the salary, thinking I'd say that's not enough, but as far as I was concerned it was three times more than I'd received the year before!

I'd only shared the impression I'd had from that first Spring Harvest with Kande, and was amazed to see God take me into BYFC without any effort or scheming on my part. I knew deep in my heart that it was the right step to take. But at the same time I tried to be reasonable and rational, so consulted several friends and advisors. Kande's reaction was positive. As well as attending that first interview with Steve, we were invited to Cleobury Place to meet the other leaders and their wives. A few days after my M61 meeting with Rob, on the morning we set off for Zimbabwe, I phoned to accept the job.

After Zimbabwe I had a two weeks stint in Portugal to help with the International Year of Youth, so I couldn't start work until November 1985, although I did attend the AGM and the opening of Cleobury Place which had just been taken over by BYFC. I'm not good at one-liners, but each member of the leadership team had to stand up at the AGM to say something about their area of the work. Each of the others made everyone laugh with their quips, so I was worried about coming across as boring. Fortunately, they were all wearing three-piece grey suits and I was dressed much more casually as my youth worker role allowed, so I said: 'I'm Lowell Sheppard, the Director of Evangelism, but I haven't started yet and that's why I haven't been issued with my uniform.' Kande heaved a sigh of relief that I'd been able to get an equal amount of laughs; it was a really good bonding experience.

I started in November and my first day was spent in a leadership team meeting talking about salary policy for three hours. I thought 'What am I doing here?' But it was a good introduction as it gave me a glimpse of some of the practical aspects of leadership. My mandate was to liberate the other evangelists, providing pastoral care and co-ordination for the work of evangelists like Cliff Meads, Phil Rowlands, Roy Crowne, Garry Gibbs, Clive Davenport, the band Alphabet and all the associate evangelists. Getting such a diverse and gifted group to work together as a team was liking riding a bucking broncho, but I saw it as a challenge.

Rob also asked me to put a priority on developing a strategy document, answering the question: 'How do we reach eight million young people with the Gospel in Britain today?' That encompassed all the teenagers in Britain. I knew God had called me to Britain when I was in Mexico, but I also felt it was strategic. If we could see a spiritual awakening among British young people it would have global implications. Britannia may no longer rule the waves, but it does rule the airwaves. Britain's music industry affects the values of young people across the globe. Hearing God's heartbeat for Britain's youth and following his footsteps to reach them was a challenge with global implications. But before God gave me any steps forward on that score, Kande and I had to go through the hardest trial of our lives so far.

14

The valley of death

While Kande was in Zimbabwe during 1985 she wondered if she was pregnant, so after we returned from Portugal she went for tests. When she arrived back from the doctor and announced: 'It's true, I'm pregnant!' a broad smile shot across my face; Kande says all I could do for about an hour was smile.

We had been married for five years and were positive about starting a family, but hadn't been trying for a child. Kande wasn't quite as excited about it as I was, though very much looking forward to the baby. Her reservations were probably linked to the changes that would have to be made in her life; her colour analysis work was taking off and, although she knew that a baby would make a difference to our lives, she didn't appreciate people saying, negatively, that life would never be the same again. So we began to prepare for our new member of the family and think about names.

I went to Zimbabwe in May and was concerned to hear about the nuclear fallout from Chernobyl that was spreading over northern Europe. I worried, illogically, that it might affect the baby's development, though by that stage in any pregnancy the baby is fully formed. The pregnancy was great; Kande wasn't sick for a day and everything happened on time. But when the due date arrived in June, the baby didn't come. Kande was two weeks overdue when doctors decided to admit her to hospital to have the baby induced. That started a catalogue of problems which all added up to making it a negative experience.

Kande went into the local hospital on the Tuesday and was put on a drip. On the Thursday morning she began to have contractions and, as I was in a leadership team meeting, she phoned to tell me. I went straight to the hospital and the second stage of labour started about 4pm, but the baby wasn't in the right position. So they put Kande on her side and told her not to push, which is very difficult when you're in that stage of labour as your mind and body are telling you that pushing will bring the pain to an end. The hospital staff tried to manoeuvre the baby which was a very bad experience for Kande; watching my wife in that amount of pain was hard for me too.

As well as the discomfort of giving birth, our surroundings were less than perfect. The hospital was very crowded and we were in a very small delivery room. The ramp at the entrance to the building was literally five feet away and, because it was a hot summer day with temperatures in the eighties, the window separating us from that thoroughfare was open. Although there was a curtain over the window anyone passing could hear what was happening. To make matters worse there was someone else giving birth literally five feet away on the other side of another curtain. There was no privacy.

Eventually the medical team decided Kande needed a forceps delivery because the baby was not turning. Five different male doctors had given Kande an internal examination by this time; the whole thing was incredibly unpleasant for her, but at least the birth was imminent.

Our first son, Luke, was born at 6.30pm on Thursday, 26 June. Seeing him for the first time was wonderful. I was immediately bonded to him. But because there had been such distress during childbirth they took him immediately to the special care baby unit which was on the edge of the hospital. In contrast to the delivery room it was completely new and one of the finest units in the West Midlands. I stayed with Kande for a few minutes then went to be with little Luke.

Kande came down to see him later and we spent some time with him before Kande went back to the ward to rest and I returned home to share the news with my mother-in-law who had come over from Canada for the birth. Although Luke was receiving special care, I thought the worst of the ordeal was over so went to bed, only to be woken again at 3.30am by my mother-in-law calling me to the telephone. I'd slept with ear plugs since childhood days in the Air-stream trailer so I hadn't heard it ring. She looked worried as she woke me saying 'It's the hospital; I think Luke is unwell.' I went to the phone, trying to wake up. The paediatrician from the special care unit told me the shocking news: 'Luke may not make it through the night; you'd best come in.'

There were no other cars on the road at that time of night so I was able to get to the hospital quite quickly. As I drove, banging my fist on the steering wheel, I went through a whole range of feelings: frightened that Luke would die; frightened that if he died I'd lose my faith; angry that God had allowed this to happen to my son and scared for Kande and how she would react. I shook my fist at God and told him it was a sick joke. He'd given us this gift and now it seemed he was taking him away. How could I trust a God who let things like this happen? It seemed grossly unfair. I was filled with emotion.

I arrived at the hospital, ran up the corridor into the special care unit. They quickly explained to me that they'd had a rough time with Luke at 1am. He had stabilised, even since they had called me, but it would be forty-eight hours before he was through the danger period. The diagnosis was that he had inhaled a massive amount of meconium during delivery. The paediatrician showed me X-rays of Luke's chest and said, 'You'll notice that only part of the heart can be seen; that's because there's so much meconium in the lungs hiding the heart.' That proved to be a wrong diagnosis. He had no meconium in his lungs and there was no heart to be seen on that side anyway. All the therapy he received over the next three days was based on an incorrect diagnosis. The nurses kept saying: 'He's got a strong heart' as his heart kept beating regularly. They nick-named him Rocky because of his fortitude. To treat him they beat his back vigorously, trying to loosen the meconium before using a tube to vacuum his lungs.

I was shown a machine that measured the level of oxygen in his blood. It indicated that Luke's lungs were not working properly; the low level of oxygen in his blood simply confirmed their diagnosis that they had to get the meconium out. All kinds of questions went through my mind about brain damage; if there was not enough oxygen for the brain, how would that affect him?

There was nothing I could do and I agreed that I wouldn't disturb Kande until she woke up naturally, so I went back home until about 6.30am. When I arrived back at the hospital the nurse went to tell Kande I was in the waiting room. She walked in, not knowing what was wrong. We sat down and I took her hand as I explained to her that things were not as we would like them to be. We cried together then walked down to the special care unit. It was then that both of us began to feel our arms aching, almost physically. We have subsequently read a book for people who have lost children through miscarriage or cot death; that almost physical sensation is one of wanting to scoop the baby up and hold him. We were denied that.

In the next three days it was as if we were on a roller-coaster. We lived hour by hour not knowing what the outcome would be. On the Friday evening they tried to put Luke on a ventilator but he fought it, so they had to sedate him. He looked dead at that point. There was a tube in his mouth and his chest was going up and down mechanically.

Kande was living moment by moment; I was constantly trying to assess the implications, thinking 'What's around the corner?' 'What if he doesn't regain consciousness?' 'If he's not going to recover from this, who makes the decision to turn the ventilator off?'

On the Saturday he was on the ventilator for most of the day. As the news spread, friends began phoning from all around the country. Countless visitors came to the hospital as they could see Luke through the windows without coming into the special care unit. That Saturday evening Steve and Janet Gaukroger came up from Stopsley Baptist Church to pray for Luke with Rob and Marion White (of BYFC). Then on Sunday morning he began to improve. I was so thankful that I drove to three local churches with the news as I knew that they had all been praying. At each church I stopped only long enough to tell the stewards at the door: 'Luke is beginning to make a recovery.' Faith began to grow and I began to feel confident that Luke would be healed.

He went on improving all through the day. I was looking for any thread of hope that I could hang on to; the medical experts were telling us all they thought we needed to know but I was desperate for as much information as possible. I sat glued to the machine that showed the oxygen level in his blood. Every time it went up one percentage point, I was exuberant, but every time it dropped I was depressed. Finally the nurses turned the monitor off because we were looking at it rather than Luke.

As he began to improve, the oxygen level seemed to be improving as well. He came off the ventilator on Sunday morning and finally at 4.30pm we took him out of the incubator and fed him. Kande changed him and we both held him and Kande was advised to start expressing her milk. When she went back to the ward for tea, I stayed an hour with Luke. He was on his side in the incubator so I got quite close. A baby's range of vision is quite short, but I was close enough for him to see me. He grabbed hold of my finger; it really was a precious hour as it felt as if there was communication between us as father and son.

I then went home to get something to eat, but at 6.15pm, Kande called me, her voice trembling: 'Lowell, come quickly. I think he's dying.' It was a real shock. Everything else that day had indicated that he was getting better. I raced to the hospital, left the car parked illegally and ran up the corridor. As I turned the corner, there was Kande standing in her blue night gown. Luke had just died. They had tried to revive him without success.

We hugged and walked slowly over to the little flat in the special care unit which is available for parents. As we sat crying Kande was pleading with God to bring Luke back to life. Then they brought him in. Initially Kande didn't want to hold him, but her arms went out instinctively; she took him in her arms as we continued praying. As we held him we slowly accepted the agonizing fact that our new-born baby had died. We knew he was still our son, but we also knew there was no life left in him.

When the doctor came in, he was crying. He told us he had recently lost his own baby at just a few months old. Knowing that was helpful. We felt he could share our pain and we were grateful that he had been open with us.

I had rushed out of the house only telling my mother-in-law 'He's dying'. She had phoned my parents who were staying at Tony Stone's house and eventually they joined us at the hospital. It was a very emotional time for us all. Of course the whole evening was spent in tears. We had a deep sense of shock. Once we got home the phone started to ring and cards started arriving. I phoned Rob and Marion right away and they helped by getting the news around to people. They also offered to come over and answer the phone and the door for us and were a great support.

We were now in uncharted territory. Kande had been pregnant. She'd given birth, but there was no child, only an empty cot at home. Kande had also endured the physical pain of the delivery and was constantly reminded of her physical and psychological preparation for motherhood. Once she began expressing milk her body had started producing more, but once Luke died she wasn't allowed to express any more as that would only perpetuate the problem. Until her body stopped producing milk, even the slightest brush against her caused her pain. She had a lot more to deal with than I did.

That evening we talked openly; losing a child can create an incredible bond. We were able to talk quite intimately and openly. Kande's pilgrimage through grief and mine sometimes overlap but we were different over the weeks and months that followed. It was Kande who said we had a choice to make. She felt that Satan was making a bid for our lives and futures and we had to make a decision: we could either continue to serve and trust God or we could dismiss him from being important in our lives. We made a conscious decision that night: despite the confusion, anger, pain and mystery, we would continue to trust God with our future and we would trust that he knew what was best for us. We had to trust him without knowing answers to questions like 'Why didn't he heal?' and 'Why did he let this happen?'

We heard later that the Hollybush Fellowship in North Yorkshire where we'd lived for three years, began their Sunday evening meeting at 6.30pm and Kate Jinadu, a friend from York who attends the fellowship, felt the church should pray for us. She felt we were caught in a battle and that the powers of darkness were vying for our futures. For the next hour, the hour in which Luke died, the hundred adults who make up the Hollybush Fellowship set aside what they had planned to do that night to pray for us. At about 7pm Kate, the wife of Paul Jinadu the evangelist, had a picture of Luke going to heaven and the angels praising God and celebrating. The meeting then changed gear as the whole fellowship began to praise God. They didn't know what had happened until later, but God had given his insight to those people 170 miles away. Their prayers supported us through the battle.

Of course our own church was praying for us as well. Our minister came round to visit and he shared something very helpful. He read Psalm 36:7 'How priceless is your unfailing love! Both high and low men find refuge in the shadow of your wings.' He explained that, often, being close to God means living on his shadowy side. As I've reflected on that I've realised that while there certainly isn't an evil side to God there is a dark side which we don't understand, but even there I can say I trust God.

We decided that we would trust God. And we trusted him with our emotions too. We were angry with him. We held him responsible, but I felt a wonderful security with that. It was like a little toddler coming up to his daddy when dad has said he can't have something and the toddler hammers his fists on his dad's knees. His daddy doesn't respond with his fists nor does he answer the question 'why?', but he embraces the child and gives him security. I felt that way. Although I was angry and confused, I felt God close, sheltering me.

We had all kinds of letters and cards and phone calls. The ones from Christians usually started out 'Words cannot express . . .' But usually their words did express their feelings and every card was meaningful; we only received one or two that were unhelpful. The non-Christians, like our neighbours, struggled with our loss. They didn't know how to relate to us, but some visitors commented on the peace in our home, even though they didn't know our source of peace. We prayed that God's peace would come, even although we were angry and crying; we weren't being heroic or anything, we were just working our way through it. The peace of God did come. The midwife who visited Kande said she dreaded coming to the house, but when she arrived she was aware of the incredible peace; she'd never felt it before.

We were advised to let our emotions show, so when we felt like crying we cried rather than internalise it. We made a decision that no matter who was around us, if we felt tears, we'd let the tears come. We cried lots but also found that the tears released laughter and joy. We had times of great hilarity during those dark and painful days.

I went into management mode to some extent as there was a funeral to organise. Marion White kindly offered to make initial contact with the funeral director and crematorium and I had to make a conscious effort to step back from managing what was going on to make sure that I was free to express my emotions.

We had the cremation service on the Thursday and a thanksgiving service at Cleobury Place. It was a small cremation service with Jim Wilkinson from Hollybush with his wife Cynthia, Cyril Baker, our pastor, Steve and Janet Gaukroger, Rob and Marion White, Bob and Jackie Reynolds plus my Mum and Dad and Kande's Mum who had been over for Luke's birth. Of course it was a very painful day. We went to Cleobury Place afterwards and Steve preached a remarkable message which has been exceedingly helpful to us since. People came from all over the country and many sent cards and letters sharing the pain with us. We were overwhelmed by their support.

After the funeral life had to go on. Hotelier David Evans offered Kande, my mother-in-law and I a holiday in Cornwall which was helpful and a good time for us. It was a good holiday, but we were faced with a decision about going back to visit our family in Canada. We had planned a trip to coincide with the birth of my brother's first child at the end of July. We had booked our tickets, but were apprehensive about seeing everyone at such a vulnerable time. However we decided to go.

At the time Kande's uncle was vice-president of Wardair and, unknown to us, he had found out about Luke's death and had made special arrangements for our trip. When we arrived at Manchester Airport a lady came up to us at the back of the queue of about 60 people and asked if we were Mr and Mrs Sheppard. She then led us to front row seats with special care all the way to Canada. I looked at the stewardess's sheet of instructions and saw our row number and name with the words: 'Don't mention baby'. They showed great sensitivity to us.

We had a great reunion with the family back in Canada but we didn't want to sour Brent and Tracy's experience. They invited us to attend the birth of their child, so we went with them and when Tracy went into labour we waited in a side room. We were the first to go in after little Tiffany was born and, although we had been anxious that it would bring back awful memories, it was a tremendous experience; there was nothing negative about it. Obviously it reminded us of Luke but it was positive and good for all of us.

We returned from Canada and had to go back to the hospital where Luke had died to hear the post mortem results. As before, it was very busy and overcrowded. When we arrived we had to stand waiting for twenty minutes outside the delivery room where Kande had given birth. Then we were ushered into a room and Kande was told to undress and get up on the table. A doctor then came racing in; you could tell he was busy and we were just another unit to deal with that day. He examined Kande briefly, looked at his file and said 'You can go now Mrs . . .' calling Kande by a completely different name.

I immediately said we were not the so-and-sos and then explained we were there to find out the results of the post mortem. At which point he looked embarrassed and turned angrily to the nurse, ordering her to go and get Kande's file. He didn't even say he was sorry, he was so embarrassed he wanted to get everything over as quickly as possible. After asking Kande a few questions, he told her she was alright and said we could go. When I asked about the results, he could only say we needed to see someone else. A few days later we saw the doctor who had carried out the post mortem. He informed us that there was no meconium in Luke's lungs beyond the usual amount you would expect to find after a normal birth. The reason his heart couldn't be seen was because he had a hypoplastic left side of the heart; it was almost non-existent.

It was a miracle that he lived as long as three days when his chest was being beaten so vigorously to dislodge the non-existent meconium. He shouldn't have lived more than a few minutes after being separated from Kande.

Up until that point Kande had been partly blaming herself for Luke's death and we'd both been blaming the hospital for ineptitude; that's not a charge against them but it was how we felt about the crowded conditions of the delivery room. We hadn't known who or what to blame, but when we discovered that he had a congenital heart defect, suddenly there was only one person we could hold responsible and that was God. Because we had decided to trust him, we were able to cope with Luke's death much more easily after that. For Kande to have carried guilt or for us to have held the hospital responsible would have been unbearable. So for both of us there was great healing and acceptance at that point. Truth is liberating.

Kande and I have cried since and have gone through different stages of grief like anger, despair, questioning and acceptance. We are constantly coming to terms with the fact that our first son is in heaven. Kande and I have not always been at the same place at the same time in the grieving process, so we have found communication to be very important. Occasionally something will still cause one or other of us to erupt into tears.

We have counselled people since, although I told God on the way to the hospital when I first realised Luke was likely to die: 'I don't want this simply to become a sermon illustration that I can talk about. I want my son alive.' We have spoken at a Spring Harvest seminar on grief and bereavement, but we don't feel that God has called us to that ministry. We're just ordinary people who've suffered, and because of that we can empathise with others who are suffering; we don't see ourselves as experts.

Luke's death has done many things for me. The two that stand out most are that it has resulted in a greater personal wholeness. His birth gave vent to a love that I never thought I had, but then his death gave me an experience of pain that I'd never had before. As a consequence I laugh and cry more easily than I once did. I enjoy life and I respect death more as well.

I've also learned mystery abounds and I cannot fully understand God. If everything about him was simple, as we sometimes suggest it is, God probably would only have written a three-page tract with three or four basic propositions on it and a few cartoon characters. But the Bible itself is so complicated and sophisticated. Yes, it's true that even a child can enter into the kingdom of God, but this never-ending discovery of truth has become part of my experience as a direct result of Luke's death. The Bible has pages of thousands of years of theology, philosophy, history and painful biography and it still doesn't capture all there is to know about God. We wrap God up in our evangelical, doctrinal packages and there's so much of him that is beyond our comprehension. I believe that even through eternity we will be discovering the truth about God. Faced with the mystery which surrounds God, there is also the gift of faith that he gives us and the mystery of his grace that enables us to believe and to trust him completely.

I had one person who came to me and said: 'If only we'd had more faith then Luke wouldn't have died.' But the Sunday he died I did have faith to believe Luke would be healed. There was not a doubt in my mind; but as he did die I have to accept the fact that his death was God's choice. At the same time I haven't stopped praying for people who are sick because the Bible says: 'You don't have because you don't ask.' I believe in healing, but I know that, ultimately, God in his mysterious sovereignty makes his decisions. I wish I could have learned these lessons about God in other ways and maybe still have Luke, but I'm very glad for all that I've learned. We're just two out of billions of people who have learned through suffering. Our experience has added to my growing conviction that only those who have experienced some form of pain or suffering can truly understand what the kingdom of God is about.

God promises: 'Blessed are those who mourn for they will be comforted.' And we did find comfort and fresh hope for the future. We were assured that a hypoplastic heart was not hereditary and was not likely to occur in any future children. Kande conceived again nine months after Luke's death and we were thrilled at the news. The due date was December 12th and the pregnancy was good with no problems. But then December 12th came and went and she was overdue again; were we going to go through a repeat of Luke's delivery?

Kande's doctor had transferred her to another hospital this time because of the bad memories. When she was a week overdue I went with her to the hospital and of course all the feelings came back with the question: 'Where is this going to end?' The doctor said we should wait at home for a few more days and if the baby didn't come after that, birth would be induced.

Christmas Eve came and Kande's parents were with us together with Tony and Sheila Stone. Kande began to have contractions during tea and was discreetly writing down times. As Sheila left she asked how far apart they were! It was not difficult to guess that labour had started. At 11.30pm that night I took Kande to the hospital; her contractions were then a few minutes apart, but when we arrived they subsided. We went up to the ward and Kande got into bed, while I lay on the floor nearby. At about 2.30am her waters broke and I ran to get the nurses who wheeled the bed out of the ward and into the lift. I got into the lift with her and they threw a packet in with me as the lift doors shut. They said they'd meet me downstairs – the pack was in case the lift got stuck! But we made it to the delivery room and at 3.30am Ryan was born after a short delivery. It was Christmas morning.

I went home to bring my parents-in-law in to see their new grandson and when we arrived we were told that both Kande and Ryan could come home with us. They were home in time for Christmas dinner. We put Ryan under the Christmas tree and took dozens of pictures of him. It really was special: having taken Luke the previous year, God had given us a very special Christmas present who shared the birthday of God's only son Jesus.

Our third son, Mackenzie Lowell, was born nearly three years later on October 22nd, 1990. Whereas Ryan looks like his dad, Mackenzie looks just like Kande's mum. Both boys are precious gifts and we are enjoying every day of their lives with us.

15

Hope for the future

In the days which followed Luke's death we drew closer
to God as well as to each other. And it was during that
time that God began to speak to me about reaching
Britain's eight million teenagers. I knew that it had to be
the Holy Spirit's work. We could calculate mathematical
strategies about reaching some this year, more the next
year, and so on. But that would leave out the supernatural
work of the Holy Spirit. The starting point had to be
prayer, but prayer would be just the beginning.

The strategy that developed had four points: Prayer,
Penetration, Proclamation and Preservation. As well as
praying we need to penetrate the youth culture,
proclaiming the Gospel with integrity. It is useless to lob
messages into the youth context; we need to get into the
culture, in the same way that Jesus became part of our
human culture; God incarnate. Our proclamation needs
to demonstrate Jesus to people with words and actions; only
by living out the Gospel can we communicate effectively.
Finally, we need to be committed to discipleship or
preserving the harvest. Youth for Christ's mission
statement calls us to disciple young people into the church.

When we returned from Canada and got back into the
work of BYFC, I presented the four-point strategy. BYFC

began to stimulate a prayer movement among young people. We prayed individually and as a leadership team; the whole movement was challenged to pray and we encouraged others to pray with us. We immediately reshaped our leadership team meetings devoting two hours of every second Tuesday morning to prayer. Since then we've had seasons of prayer within BYFC and have launched the Warrior initiative which is now under the auspices of the Evangelical Alliance and draws on the insights of ten other youth movements.

The fresh emphasis on prayer was the start of a new era in BYFC, but there were major hurdles on the horizon. At the end of the eighties we became aware that the movement was heading into financial difficulties. We had given no emphasis to fund-raising and had continued to grow as opportunities for ministry opened up. New ministry opportunities were continually becoming apparent, so although income was growing, expenditure had overtaken income. The board recognised this and realised that the movement needed someone to take the money situation in hand. I was asked to become Director of Finance. Apart from my excursions into financial matters in Thailand, I had little experience. I was unfamiliar with budgets and balance sheets and was helped by John Rogers who sacrificially gave of his time to work with me in getting a measure of our financial problems. We calculated that by March 1989 we were going to have a shortfall of £100,000.

We launched a crisis fund-raising strategy and by March 31, 1989 we had seen about £98,000 come in from about twenty contacts. However that fuelled our problem as about half of that money was from interest-free loans which needed to be repaid, but at least they gave us the time we needed to determine the roots of our problems. Some of the difficulties quickly became apparent: we had grown too fast; we were going to lose a large amount of income from a single source; we had no strategy for fund-raising; the computer was churning out accounts which were three months old; the team didn't have financial management skills and we had been lax in keeping a reign on our financial structures.

We began by addressing each of these problems. We were given a gift of £40,000 to buy a new computer system. We hired a fund-raiser whose first year's salary was paid by a trust, and he established a long-term strategy for us. We also set up Director's Circle to recruit businessmen and professionals, not only to give £20 a month to the work, but to give their skills. In the first year we recruited twenty-nine people to Director's Circle, including financial advisers and a qualified accountant who became our new national treasurer.

Meanwhile the recession had started and our debts were mounting. By spring 1991 we found ourselves in debt to the bank to the tune of £400,000, all of that in overdraft; also £200,000 was owed to private lenders and we were on 60 days credit with suppliers. The debt included money owed by BYFC as well as its subsidiary Cleobury Place Trust Ltd. The new BYFC centre near Kidderminster, Cleobury Place, was the main problem. We had bought it for approximately £200,000 and had spent about £500,000 refurbishing it; we still owed about £325,000 of that and, although we had the site up and running, it still needed massive investment. We didn't know where to turn. As a board and leadership team we spent hours repenting and taking corrective action.

We did see miraculous provision as God brought in the initial £98,000; the computer was replaced and we were able to pay staff on time on all but two occasions. But we were unable to increase staff salaries in line with inflation and we had to go through two waves of redundancies. This was the hardest task of all, telling faithful workers we could no longer afford their position. That was bad enough but we still had to get out of debt which was increasing each month. It was a very difficult time for the whole team. How do you let someone go when God called them to be with you? But when there's no money to pay their salary what do you do? We asked if God had left the work, but there was no sense that he had. We felt we were under God's disciplining hand and his discipline was painful.

Finally we realised that we were not equipped for the burden of managing a large conference centre with over 200 beds. We wanted to keep our focus on evangelism, so began to ask God to show us a way forward. We had close links with the Northamptonshire Association of Youth Clubs and, as Rob White met with John Whittaker, the association's chief executive officer, they began to discuss one another's strengths. They concluded that BYFC's strength was running evangelistic youth programmes and NAYC's strength, as a Christian organisation but not an evangelistic one, was running centres for young people – they already had four centres. John was a member of the BYFC board and, during 1990, he took a much more hands-on role in directing the centre alongside his other work.

By this time I was having regular meetings with the bank manager. He should have pulled the plug on us, and there was pressure on him to do so, but he seemed to believe in what we were doing. We explored every option and again, in May 1991, the board asked God's forgiveness for ever going into overdraft. We decided never to live in overdraft again. On a weekly basis you have to allow for cash flow, but that's very different from living in overdraft. I felt the pressures particularly intensely as I had been living closer than most to the figures; I'd also led the way on the redundancy programmes, but that board meeting seemed like a turning point.

Within a few days God prompted Rob White to phone the man who had helped supply the computer. He had helped finance other youth centres so Rob told him about our problem. We had heard that his trust was interested in buying a youth centre in the Midlands so we invited him to look at Cleobury Place; we could see no way out other than to sell it. Rob's phone call started a chain of events. Rob's contact decided to lend us the money to pay off the bank overdraft, but only if we could demonstrate that we could manage the centre. He could see we were gifted evangelists but he wasn't sure about our property management skills. We agreed that NAYC would manage the centre as they had a proven track record. They concluded that they could only manage it if they owned it. So we entered into a partnership with them whereby they would buy the centre from us, using the loan from the third party, but it would remain the home of BYFC.

NAYC would run the centre; we would run our programmes; the solution was better than we could have hoped. Instead of having access to just one centre, we'd have access to all the NAYC centres. Also, we would retain a ten-year lease on the BYFC offices, for a peppercorn rent. All this happened over a period of three or four months. In late October 1991 we completed the deal; paid the bank off in full. Private loans have nearly all been repaid as well so, when Rob handed over the job of national director in July 1992, BYFC was completely out of debt to the bank and private loans had been reduced from £200,000 to £60,000.

Now BYFC is re-focusing itself on the task of winning the nation's young people to Christ. It is not a Cleobury-centred movement, though that is the administrative centre and we are committed to residential experiences for young people. We now feel a strong sense of God's guiding hand on the movement. Since being released from the burden of debt and from managing a large conference centre, we have been applying ourselves to vision and strategy. Director's Circle has brought much-needed professional gifts to the movement. Two particular men have helped us strategically: Mike Smith, managing director of an engineering firm, gave a lot of time to assist us through our crisis, and Peter Bishop, a well-experienced consultant, has given one day a week to us throughout 1992 as we have planned for the future.

Our vision is to take the Good News relevantly to every young person in Britain. The strategy we are working on will answer the question: How?

It has been encouraging to see the whole movement become engaged in the process of strategic planning. We have identified six core values which we want to be hallmarks of YFC in the '90s: Prayer Power; Preaching; Pioneering; Partnership; Professionalism; Person-centred.

The movement is motivated to work the vision through. Richard Eyre, Managing Director of Capital Radio, hosted the launch of our new corporate identity. He described YFC's vision for the '90s as refreshing and relevant. We have a serious determination to achieve the vision. We are seeking thousands of partners who will stand with YFC in our future. I'm glad for all God has given me to do over the years. But I feel as if I'm just beginning.

BYFC is concerned with the wider world as well. I was one of the team leading the English delegation to Lausanne II in Manila in 1989. This gathering of 4,000 Christian leaders met to discuss global evangelisation and, like most conferences, awful was mixed with brilliant. I was particularly challenged by men like Bible teacher Ajith Fernando and evangelist John Smith, who was cold-shouldered by the conference as he lived out the Gospel practically, opposing injustice and ending up in a Filipino jail! Most of all the conference challenged me to be always outlooking, seeking ways to take the Good News in word and deed to young people.

With hindsight, I can see how God has been preparing me for my new role in BYFC. I was frightened to death about the change of leadership, but also felt a deep sense of God's call towards it. And, if nothing else, I've learned that God does equip those he calls. In financial matters, my faith has grown as I've seen God's provision from the Zimbabwe fares and the Montego, to the creative way God has turned BYFC's finances around. The experience as Director of Finance taught me that financial management isn't merely common sense, it's an act of spiritual warfare. As I've studied Scripture I see that money was Jesus' second favourite subject, after the Kingdom of God. He talked about money in terms of allegiance: 'You cannot serve both God and money' (Matthew 6:24). The Bible shows that money is a form of power that imbeds itself in people's souls. It's so easy for our allegiance to switch from God to money. Financial managers tame the power of money so it flows into the Kingdom of God for his use. I now look at accountants in a new light; they must have a spiritual calling, as spiritual gifts are needed to wage war with Mammon – the money god. Even fund-raising is an act of spiritual warfare. It means going out and claiming what belongs to God. As National Director I feel it is part of my calling to present the vision of youth evangelism and to raise the money to do it.

I am grateful for a good team who work with me, leading the movement. Eddie Lyle, Roy Crowne, Dennis Birch and Maggie Everett, each bring distinctive gifts and impressions. We don't always agree, but we are committed to work as a team. The Board of Leadership of YFC are determined for the movement to grow, and not to forget the lessons of recent years.

But where does this leave me in my efforts to merge social action and evangelism? My first conversion, as a teenager, came as I became convinced that Christ is the answer to the world's need. My second conversion took place after God softened my heart towards the world's poor, trapped without choice or opportunity to change. The third conversion was to draw evangelism and social action together in a green revolution.

16

A third conversion – a green one!

When Ajith Fernando, the National Director of YFC in Sri Lanka, came to the BYFC staff conference in 1988 he led a series of Bible studies on friendship from the book of Proverbs. But he also ran a special session on the New Age movement. Weaving through it all was an attitude towards God and his creation which I found fascinating as well as Biblical. He demonstrated the differences between Western and Eastern cultures, highlighting the elements of Buddhism and Hinduism which we cannot write-off as being un-Biblical. In every false religion there are elements of truth; in the East there is a greater emphasis on the natural realm, even Eastern Christians put less emphasis on time and more on caring for the environment and nurturing healthy relationships.

I left the conference struck by the need for Christians to be concerned about God's world. Ajith particularly challenged us in the West to repent of our busy-ness and to learn to linger, enjoying God's creation; and secondly to repent of our utilitarian attitudes which we justify with Scriptures.

Two months later I was on my way to ski in the Alps with MasterSki and I read a Newsweek article about the animal rights movement in the USA. For the first time I felt real concern and offence at some of our practices with animals in the name of science, medicine and cosmetics; not that I suddenly leapt on the bandwagon and joined an animal rights group, but it did something to tenderise me as I realised in a deeper way that God does love his entire creation. We are different from animals and plants as human beings are made in God's image but God loves this world, as outlined in John 3:16. It literally means 'God loved the cosmos', so it's not just humanity which is showered with his love; he loves his creation; all that he has made.

That Newsweek article started me on a road of reflection, prayer and study. Also, I began to explore the New Age movement more than I had, because of its influence on young people. I came to the conclusion that the New Age movement has hijacked a number of areas where we, as the church, need to regain our cutting edge. There are three main allies of the New Age movement: the Peace movement, the Feminist movement and the Green movement. Christians can find Biblical justification to be involved in all three of those.

It is abundantly clear that we should be seekers of peace. The Feminist movement is controversial, though I know which side I take on that in terms of liberation, allowing women to take their full role in the church. I believe there is no male and female in Christ. We need both male and female perspectives in ministry and leadership. And on the environmental issue, the church has built its theology on God's command in Genesis 1:28: '. . . fill the earth and subdue it.' We have developed that and exploited the Earth, taking everything we can out of it whereas, in fact, we need to take into account the rest of Scripture which places a value upon creation and the fact that God made it for his pleasure.

As I began to probe the New Age movement, I realised that many people were being sucked into this heretical understanding of God, an Eastern mystical understanding whereby God is in nature. They buy into a Star Wars theology and believe that God is not a person but a force and to get back to God we must get back to nature. It feels good and right, so a lot of Christians are being duped by this heresy. True Christians need to declare this is God's world and because we are his we are going to care for it.

Modern day environmentalists all find their roots in 19th century Christian thinking. Some bordered on pantheism and began to leave the Christian faith, but John Muir, for example, founded the Sierra Club, out of which came Friends of the Earth. Muir had Presbyterian roots and no doubt his understanding of Scripture helped shape his concern for the environment. Christians cannot write-off environmental concerns as 'New Age' and yet many Christians are concerned about New Age ideas affecting them if they 'go Green'.

My pilgrimage on this is still going. As a family we are not yet Green in the way that we live. We are trying to work things through at a practical level, dividing rubbish for example. Kande and the boys had fun by ceremoniously placing an empty milk bottle into the toilet cistern, thus conserving one litre each time we flush the loo. We also now use low wattage light bulbs. But it had to start at a philosophical level before it began to affect our lifestyle. It has answered the dilemma I've been living with as I've realised that my dilemma was one of false dualism. The reason I felt split in my ministry towards social action and towards preaching the Gospel, is because of this ingrained teaching that I'd received that it is only eternity that really matters. We split God from the natural realm and compartmentalise a lot saying God is not interested in how I fill out my expense form, for example, or God isn't really with us when we go and enjoy the opera. That's the extreme and logical conclusion of dualism. I realised that I'd been living subject to dualistic thinking. I didn't want to but it was so ingrained in me, I felt torn. My heart went out to the poor, but my mind told me: 'Preach the Gospel.' As I began to study Scripture and look at the New Age movement, things have become more whole for me. The natural realm, including the arts and culture, have taken on a new significance. God actually enjoys these things.

What also pushed me over the edge was an episode of the BBC programme QED, called the 'Song of the Skylark'. David Hindley, a Cambridge music master in his retirement years, studied the dawn chorus using sophisticated equipment to record bird-song and transpose it into a musical score to be played by a digital key-board. The highlight of his project had been the song of the skylark. He had recorded forty-eight seconds of a skylark's song then slowed the tape down sixteen times as, on average, the bird sang two hundred distinct notes per second. The BBC panel of experts who analysed the work found one similarity after another when they compared the skylark's song with Beethoven's Fifth Symphony. They said that the similarity in notes must be sheer coincidence. What intrigued them most were the patterns and musical principles which were nearly identical to those of Beethoven. They concluded by giving two options: either the skylark has evolved from the same reptile as humanity and shares the same brain stem so a skylark's appreciation of music will be much the same as a human being's, or, they said, this is the closest thing to the music of heaven that we'll ever hear on earth. It is a powerful illustration that God's fingerprints are everywhere.

C.S. Lewis pointed out that Christians drain nature of its divinity, asserting that nature is not God, but we haven't taken on board the truth that nature is an index of who God is; it points to God. The whole of the universe is God's cathedral. For me, it came as a revelation that the 'Now' matters as well as the future. I began to feel God's tenderness for his creation; God is concerned about major oil disasters which kill fish, plants and birds. It is not a cop out to 'Go Green' as it gives rightful respect to the environment which is God's property.

At Spring Harvest in 1989 I was to speak for fifteen minutes on the Passion of Christ; I spoke about Christ's heart breaking for young people, for the church and for the planet. I stated that, if anyone should be leading the way on the environment, it should be Christians. In the weeks after that God seemed to say, 'Why don't you do something about it?' I hadn't expected to preach on that subject again but God seemed to be challenging me, although, as we've integrated the environmental challenge into the programme, Spring Harvest has had some criticism for shifting our focus away from the Gospel when people are going to hell. To me that argument is a cop-out as it ignores the Biblical imperative of stewardship and a proper understanding of God's love for creation.

Some suggest that to be conscious of the environment is to adopt New Age thinking, but I believe that is simple evangelical paranoia. Steve Chalke, of the Oasis Trust, once described the New Age movement as a luxury liner: it has a lot of good things on board, but it's not what's on board that should concern us, but what direction the liner is going. It is true that the New Age movement has many elements which should concern Christians, but it points to human beings as gods, rather than taking us closer to the one true God. That's where Christians are different.

There are a number of good Biblical reasons why we should be concerned for the environment, primarily because God says that creation is good. American sociologist Tony Campolo gave an excellent illustration at a Youth for Christ rally when he imagined God creating a daisy. God saw it was good and said: 'Do it again!' So he made another daisy . . . and another . . . and another, until he had made millions of daisies . . . and he was still saying to himself: 'Oh, I like it. Do it again!' Creation is good. God says it.

Secondly, we need to face the issue of stewardship. When environmentalists talk about stewardship they are often thinking in terms of taking care of all that belongs to our children. Although this is legitimate, there is a much stronger case for stewardship and that is the Biblical one. The world was created by God and for God; it belongs to him and we must be good stewards of its resources, caring for its beauty and balance.

Thirdly, as the Bible leans towards the poor, we also need to be concerned for the world's poor who are often the most affected by the environmental crisis. Vast areas of Africa are ploughed up to plant cash crops for sale in the affluent West; ancient trees in the Far East are torn down to make valuable furniture for the West; rain forests in South America are destroyed to graze cattle for Western burger bars.

Also, Christian concern for the environment must be linked to the fact that all creation praises God; it is there as a demonstration of God's glory. When an angry mob rolled into a French village during the Revolution, trying to destroy everything that reminded them of the establishment – including God – a French peasant looked up as the church was being destroyed and said: 'Go ahead; you can never remove the stars'. He had a Biblical understanding of the cathedral God has created in the heavens; all creation calls us to worship God, the Creator.

Finally, we care for the environment because Jesus said: 'God so loved the world . . .'. God sent his Son to redeem mankind, and the whole of the cosmos. God mourns over creation and Jesus has come to rescue it. He says: 'I will make all things new' and, as well as renewing his people, he will renew the world, rescuing it from sin which has spoilt all God made.

As I began to understand this I could see the challenge to dualism in the Church. God is interested in the eternal and the spiritual, but he is also interested in the temporary: the Now! As I discussed these issues with friends and colleagues there came an idea to develop a project which would allow young people at Spring Harvest to bridge the gap between now and eternity.

Spring Harvest's young people have always given offerings for different causes, but for Spring Harvest 1991, we felt that we should have a single focus for the youth offerings. One Sunday morning when I was at church a whole concept seemed to fall into place about focusing the attention of young people at Spring Harvest on an environmental issue. I'd had no contact with Burkina Faso for years and I had a growing sense that God wanted me to do something there again but I didn't know what. I did know that traumatic environmental changes had been taking place in the southern Sahara affecting the whole country. I also knew that Youth for Christ had started up there. So I phoned John Jacques Weiler, the European Director of YFC who had helped get Burkina Faso YFC off the ground. He put me into touch with Michele Ouedrago, Chairman of YFC in Burkina Faso, who told me of their three-fold strategy: evangelism, education and ecology. They felt that all three were part of the mission of Christ within their region. I was deeply challenged by this: we were arguing about it; they were doing it. As well as reaching their people through evangelism, quenching their spiritual thirst, they were working to make a difference to the environment of their drought-ravaged country. They wanted to plant trees to fight the desert which was growing at a rate of three kilometres a year. So I asked if Spring Harvest could join forces with them to help find the funds to plant the trees. We were encouraged by the enthusiastic response the Spring Harvest executive gave to the proposal, particularly Colin Saunders the chairman.

Within a week, the main building blocks for the project had come together. We were to send a TV crew to film the problem, then we would show five minute clips each night at Spring Harvest, to educate the young people. Then on the final day they would raise funds and take up offerings. Our target was £25,000 and, as the most we'd ever raised before was £8,000, it was an ambitious goal. We didn't want to spend money on administration but Spring Harvest donated some of the offerings from their autumn tour to get the team to Burkina Faso to film the video. We also wrote to UTA, the French airline which flies into Ouagadougou, the capital of Burkina Faso. The British general manager of the airline phoned my assistant,

Rachael Orrel the next day to say they'd love to be involved. They were willing to reduce the fares for the film crew by eighty per cent. We then went to CVG Television who offered to give their services free of charge.

Eddie Lyle, a fellow YFC leader and myself along with a CVG film crew spent a week filming in Burkina Faso in December 1990, visiting Michele Ouedrago to see the YFC work as well as my friends Clark and Rob Lungren who arranged the wildlife shots. We arrived to find that the cameras had been lost in transit. One arrived eventually and we had to pick the second up in Paris on the way back as there were only a couple of flights to Burkina Faso each week. But, undaunted, we toured the country on a punishing schedule seeing YFC's work as well as the Nazinga project where the Lungren brothers have successfully reversed the desertification process. It was thrilling to see the dam which I had seen being built in 1981. The area had flooded according to plan and elephants were drinking there every day.

One of the most memorable moments was travelling north to get the desert shots. We were half way between Ouagadougou and Timbuktoo in a wilderness area which had been jungle only fifteen years before. We could see some of the dead trees which had been part of that thriving forest. It was an awesome sight. We then visited a village called Golmidou, which was to be the focus of the project. The village chief laid on a feast for us and the village dancers put on a display which made the week even more memorable. But the growth of the desert made the most impact on us. It was recommended that a dam be built before trees were planted. We agreed that the bulk of the money raised at Spring Harvest would be used for that aspect of the project.

When we showed the video, the young people at Spring Harvest really caught the vision and doubled the target by raising £49,000. The dam has now been built, the trees have been planted and Tear Fund have used the surplus money for similar projects in West Africa. It was hugely successful. The young people mixed with other age groups on the Spring Harvest sites, fund-raising in lots of chaotic ways. We always want Spring Harvest to be a catalyst to real change back home so we encouraged the young people to go back home to raise more money. That way the environmental issue could have an impact in their home communities; some did hold fund-raising events at home and a further £11,000 was raised and forwarded to Tear Fund.

Developing the Green initiative still further, the following year Spring Harvest and Tear Fund ran the Whose Earth initiative. It sought to mobilise local churches in environmental action. Launched at the Houses of Parliament by Simon Hughes MP in March 1992, it had the backing of the Archbishop of Canterbury, Martyn Joseph, Clive Calver, John Stott, Prof. G. T. Prance, the Director of Kew Gardens and Roger Forster. Whose Earth succeeded in recruiting 700 local groups to be involved in environmental action throughout the summer. It also sent a youth team to the earth summit in Rio and with the help of BYFC organised the 'Join the World' event – a day of activities in London's Hyde Park. A total of 2,300 Christians created a world record and attracted media attention by forming the largest ever people map of the globe. As cameras rolled from Capital Radio's 'eye in the sky' helicopter, the crowd shouted 'Whose Earth? God's Earth!' It was an exciting day which included the appearance of a 40 feet high earth ball, John Smith, Sal Solo, Michael Green, Roger and Faith Forster, Steve Chalke, Roy Crowne, and the sun . . . the weather was miraculous. A message was brought from the Queen while TV was covering it live.

The day was significant in the lives of all those who took part, whether they were committed environmentalists or complete novices. More than 1,000 pledged their commitment to bring about change in their lives and the lives of others by helping to get the environment into order. Together we affirmed our role as stewards rather than owners of the earth and agreed to on-going participation in local environmental action such as recycling projects, litter collection and waste ground renewal.

Huge amounts of energy were expended during the project by Grahame Dale, Gillian Smith and Rachel Orrel, who worked tirelessly for months to make the Hyde Park event happen, along with hundreds of volunteers who freely gave of their time.

For me the event demonstrated a step forward in pushing back the boundaries of Christian thinking on the subject of the environment. As Christians we can and must be concerned about whole people. But that was only one day; a small step . . . I still haven't found what I'm looking for.

17

I still haven't found what I'm looking for

As a wayward adolescent in the late '60s and early '70s, I desperately wanted to smoke hash. Funnily enough this 'burning ambition' was never realised until I had become an evangelist and had long-since lost the desire. I had been invited to speak at the Glastonbury Festival and hash was being used on the site all around me; I was a passive smoker in the crushing crowd in front of the pyramid stage on a farm under the shadow of Glastonbury Tor. The Glastonbury event is a huge home-grown music festival, organised by a farmer, attracting 100,000 people.

Glastonbury Festival illustrates for me Bruce Springsteen's perceptive comment that everyone has a 'hungry heart'. The various fields in the area the Glastonbury programme described as 'Babylon' included 'Green Field', 'Sacred Field' and 'Healing Field' – all buzzing with seekers looking for answers to life's questions.

Hope Now Ministries, under the leadership of Vic Jackopson, had 350 workers sharing Christ at the 1992 Glastonbury Festival. Among these were twenty-five YFC workers from our two mobile street teams: Streetlife and On The Edge, led by Dave Townsend and Steve Bedford along with veteran YFC evangelist, Lindsay Hamon. (Lindsay is notorious for carrying a cross through the towns and villages of Britain as he shares Christ with people.) Our YFC workers were living on site and sharing 'Good News' practically. Sadly, Hope Now Ministries were not allowed to operate out of 'Babylon' where the need was greatest. In fact, Vic has since told me that he has been banned from the festival altogether for holding an anti-pagan position.

I was asked to speak in Vic's tent on 'Christians and the Environment'. Sadly only twelve people were present, which illustrates the need for Christians to get out of the ghetto and take the risk of invading our fallen world with the Good News of Jesus. Christians need to be in the thick of the action allowing our faith to be challenged as we stand up with confidence sharing the Good News which has changed our lives and all of history. We must not let the Good News be sidelined to the fringe. We live in a confused and hurting world.

Secular futurist Alvin Toffler, in his 1970s book *Future Shock* mapped out the course of our increasingly unstable society. His thesis was that because world culture was changing at increasing speed, the whole of society would experience a form of culture shock: the same fear, depression, numbness and paranoia that can be experienced when moving from one country's culture to another would be experienced by people coping with increasingly rapid cultural changes. His prophetic insight has come true. Many people are fearful and depressed; numbed by the modern Western consumer culture which grabs more and more things which have no substance and can never satisfy. The old cliché is true: when God is emptied from society, society becomes empty.

The hippy generation quoted Nietzsche and said 'God is dead'. Having dismissed God they began searching for other solutions to the world's problems. Some said drugs were the answer, now they have LSD-induced brain damage. Many sought answers through self-expression in the arts, but the searching Sixties gave way to Punk rebellion in the Seventies and the shallowness of the

Eighties which were epitomised by Kylie Minogue's trite ditty: 'I should be so lucky'. With a few notable exceptions, even art has become disposable. Where was the church as our culture clutched at straws in its painful search for reality? We were locked in a debate over guitars in church and the evils of rock music, ignoring the plight of the generation in pain outside the closed doors of our churches. Jesus would have been in the pubs, clubs and discos touching hurting people's lives; bringing meaning, reality and wholeness.

I was on a Liverpool street corner a couple of years ago with my friend, Australian evangelist John Smith. I had just been conned out of a pound by a wino called Vincent. Ten minutes later Vincent was feeding the same sob story to John when I appeared. Vincent was cleverly adapting his tale of woe when John reached out and touched Vincent's forehead: 'Vincent, the reason you're like this is because of the pain you have up here,' John said. Then he touched Vincent's chest '. . . and the pain you have down here.' Suddenly Vincent broke into uncontrollable sobs, partly because he was inebriated, but also because a chord of reality had been struck deep in his being. The Kingdom of God had come and, for a moment, met him face to face.

Vincent came into our meeting that night in the Methodist Central Hall and I would love to report that he has since been converted and is working as an evangelist. He did come to the meeting, but he vomited and slept through most of it. Vincent encountered the Kingdom of God that night: reality with both good news and bad news. The bad news was his emptiness and pain. That will and should plague him until he steps into the Good News and becomes part of the Kingdom of God.

Sadly, the church has too often been good at highlighting the bad news in others, disregarding the bad news inside the church and forgetting to share the Good News with the world at large. It is the church's responsibility to be heralds of Good News. When the Holy Spirit comes he brings judgement; people feel bad because of injustice and sinfulness. We can rely on the Holy Spirit to do his work. The work of the church must be to bring the message of love and hope that young people desperately need to hear. Most know nothing of the true Jesus. Singer and self-publicist Madonna is quoted as saying that she wears a crucifix because she likes nude men. To Christians her comment is outrageous, but her lyrics demonstrate the cry of her generation. In 'Rescue Me' you find a bewildered and confused girl in great pain.

At a YFC gathering, Richard Eyre of Capital Radio described young people today as living in a state of emptiness. I believe that is true and caused by a dramatic loss of three vital things.

First of all we have jettisoned truth from our vocabulary. Leslie Newbiggin, who is a former missionary to India and co-general secretary of the World Council of Churches told YFC staff that this is the fundamental problem in western society. As a result young people are presented with confused and contradictory messages, they are unsure who and what to believe.

There has also been a loss of love and security. With family breakdown, the church's perceived irrelevance and rapid social changes, young people do not have the vital anchors for orientation and security.

Finally there has been loss of purpose. Life is largely meaningless for growing numbers of people, particularly those trapped by the widening poor/rich gap. Burn out is not so much caused by pace of life but rather by loss of central meaning. It would appear to me that western culture is in an advanced stage of burn out.

But there is Good News.

A few years ago I heard the Methodist Bible teacher Donald English interpret and apply Philippians 2:1–4 on the mind of Christ. He explained that the best way to understand the word 'mind' was to use three words: think, feel and do. In other words, to let the 'think, feel and do' of Christ be our 'think, feel and do'. As I have reflected on that explanation it has shaped my own understanding of what it means to be a follower of Jesus.

First of all Christians must be thinkers. I claim no great intellectual prowess, but I have found that the more I have learned about truth, about God and about his world, the greater is my enjoyment of God, truth and the world. Followers of Christ must be thinking people who grapple with issues affecting the environment, culture, politics, the arts; every area of life. We must not simply be spongeheads, absorbing films, music and television programmes without critically assessing them. There is no excuse for Christians to adopt narrow tracks of thinking, locking into narrow denominational dogmas rather than being the growing, innovative and daring thinkers that Christ died to save. And we must reject the temptation to communicate truth in ten second bursts and good sound bytes. Rather we must challenge people, and young people in particular, to ponder profound truths.

Secondly, Christians must be more than thoughtful heads, we must have feeling hearts. I am continually confronted by Bob Pierce's challenge to find out what is breaking the heart of God, then pray it breaks our hearts as well. My natural inclination is to retreat emotionally and remain detached. While we were in Croatia we discussed how the journalists cope. Many of them switch off emotionally, but that is not the way of God's Kingdom. As followers of Jesus we weep with those who weep and celebrate with those who are celebrating. The Six o'clock News challenges me to cry; to mourn for the Madonna-generation, and to pray with passion for the Kingdom of God to come. For if there is no war in heaven, we must pray passionately that there is no war on earth; if there is no abuse in heaven, we must pray fervently that there will be no abuse here on earth; if there is no famine in heaven, we must pray earnestly that there is no famine on earth.

Finally, we must not only think and feel; we must also 'do'. Psychoanalyst Sigmund Freud described religion as the crutch – or escape from reality – that some people need to get through life. That is not the way of Jesus. Freud obviously did not read the records of Jesus' life. Jesus did not stay on the Mount of Transfiguration, escaping into a mountain-top, supernatural experience. He came back down the mountain to rescue a fallen world. Jesus is recorded in Scripture as saying dozens of times: 'Come and follow me'. Following him – being like Jesus in all we do – is not a glamorous, super-spiritual experience, but an intensely practical, often dirty, sometimes dangerous adventure.

I was deeply challenged by a friend of my parents, Verle Halcrow, who fell in love with Jesus early in her adult life. She and her husband Floyd set about serving God together by raising children in the Christian faith: they had eight of their own and fostered many more. Today, many of those young people love God. Two don't. They were daughters of a prostitute who had abandoned them. After several years being cared for as part of the Halcrow family, the prostitute regained custody of the girls. Many years later, in the summer of 1990 after the Halcrows had retired, the police arrived at their home with a warrant for Verle's arrest. She was charged with child abuse. There were specific references to religious indoctrination; the girls' Christian upbringing was to be put on trial.

It came to light that the trial judge was angry with the church; his son had converted to Christianity. Verle was found guilty and that judge sentenced her to four years in prison – a decision which angered the two girls who were hoping for financial compensation. In my opinion the harsh sentence was the judge's way of getting back at the church which he so hated.

Verle was put on Death Row for her own safety. This elderly, Godly woman began telling the other inmates about Jesus. After appealing against the conviction, Verle was released on bail to await a re-trial and the judge was de-benched. Talking to her about her experiences she says she has no regrets. She was happy to follow Jesus, despite the cost. Serving and following Jesus is an adventure but it is no escape. It brings us face to face with injustice, unrighteousness and people's pain and hurt. That is true holiness; not simply signs and wonders, some form of breast-beating or an other-worldly experience. Holiness is solidly embedded in the real world, walking in the steps of Jesus.

I have struggled to write this book as I have had to examine my own motivations. I abhor the thought that I might imply that I have arrived at a satisfactory place in my pilgrimage with God. I still haven't found what I'm looking for. I see that life so far hasn't brought me to an arrival lounge but to a springboard into further adventures of discovering Christ in the world. Instead of becoming more comfortable, I find myself becoming increasingly uncomfortable, unhappy, even angry at the state this world is in. But, as I look at the increasingly troubled world, hope does not disappear. Instead hope is growing stronger as I become more certain that Christ longs to come.

We must not only pray towards God's Kingdom coming, we must work towards it. We must be the arms and legs of Jesus, implementing his plan and reflecting his tenderness. Gerard Kelly's version of the Lord's Prayer gives relevance and passion to the heart cry which I echo:

Let Your Kingdom Come

Let it break out like blisters
On the skin of this city
Let it cut to the heart
Like cardiac surgery
Let it be as deeply rooted
As cedars, touching bedrock.
Let it travel more widely
Than Zaphod Beeblebrock.
Let it be more arresting
Than the Special Patrol Group.

Let it come like Hotwheels cars
Scorching down to loop the loop.
Let it spread on the grapevine
Like a death on EastEnders
Let it cause such a stir
As a wedding on Neighbours.

Let it come like a hurricane
Like a fire, like a river.
Let it spread like a virus,
Like war, like a rumour.
Like the raising of a curtain
Like the roll of a drum,
Let it come to us,
Let your Kingdom come.

Let its landing be more welcomed
Than Michael Jackson's jet.
Let it affect more households
Than the rise of credit debt.
Let it arouse greater faith
Than the Pope, kissing tarmac.
Let it come with more relish
Than Large Fries and a Big Mac.
Let it win more accolades
Than Olivier's acting,
Let it relieve suffering
More than Botha repenting.
Let it touch as many lives
As water fluoridation,
Let it seep through more frontiers
Than Chernobyl's radiation.

Let it come like a hurricane,
Like a fire, like a river,
Let it spread like a rumour,
Like the raising of a curtain,
Like the roll of a drum.

Let it come to us,
Let your Kingdom come.
(Poem reproduced by kind permission of the author)

Western society seems to be on its last legs. The decade which started with great hope has been strangled at birth and young people are bearing the brunt of it. The coming of God's Kingdom is the only answer for our broken world and its lonely, hurting inhabitants. Christians need to play our part in overturning injustice, changing the structures which keep people oppressed. Alone we cannot bring about the necessary transformation, but as followers of Jesus we are part of a Spirit-filled, world-changing movement that does a deeper work than changing societies' structures. When God's Kingdom comes, like John Smith touching a vagrant, Jesus touches individual lives, each with their own experience of pain and fear. And in his touch healing and hope flow out in transforming power to change the world from the inside out.

Jesus has come and has set history moving in a new direction. He has begun the process of renewal, redeeming the world from the awful impact of sin. And he will come again, but until that time the church is his body here on earth, individually and collectively. Warts and all, we are the only hope the world has of hearing the Good News. Therefore, I am committed to taking that Good News to every young person in Britain. Youth for Christ, of which I am part, has the same motivation and although each church, organisation or individual has a particular angle, we each have a unique part to play. Let us all be in pursuit of the never-ending adventure, introducing others to their own adventure of life in God's hands.

The Croatian church is a challenge to us. They have begun to give their attention to the poor and, in particular, the Moslems who are the victims in that evil war. As a result the winds of renewal are sweeping through the Croatian church the Jesus way. Having seen the impact of their adventurous and risky living, I am orientating myself to step into unknown networks and secular environments. I see no dichotomy between Jesus the Christ and Jesus of Nazareth, between spirituality and liberation, between sacred and secular, between faith and works, between eternity and time, or between prayer and action. Jesus calls us simply to mimic him and be empowered by his Spirit. John Wesley was right in describing the Christian faith as a never ending adventure. Every day can be a discovery of truth, security of meaning.

We will never arrive as Christians. If you meet me and notice that I am settling down, becoming static, I invite you to ask me the question: 'How is the adventure going, Lowell?' I may then be reminded that there are no arrival lounges in God's Kingdom; the adventure with Jesus never ends.

NOTE

YFC is an international organisation, with over 60 centres in Britain. It specialises in sharing the Christian faith relevantly and responsibly with young people.

For further information about YFC, please contact them at:

Cleobury Place
Cleobury Mortimer
Kidderminster
DY14 8JG

Tel: 0224 270260

BYFC is a registered charity no. 209338.